Thermophobia
Shining a Light on Global Warming

Shining a Light Series

Dirt Ordinary: Shining a Light on Conspiracies, by Rod Martin, Jr.
Favorable Incompetence: Shining a Light on 9/11, by Rod Martin, Jr.
Thermophobia: Shining a Light on Global Warming, by Rod Martin, Jr.

Climate Basics series

Climate Basics: Nothing to Fear, by Rod Martin, Jr.—an Amazon #1 Bestseller in Weather and Science & Math Short Reads.
Deserts & Droughts: How Does Land Ever Get Water? by Rod Martin, Jr.

Thermophobia
Shining a Light on
Global Warming

Rod Martin, Jr.

Shining a Light *series*

Tharsis Highlands Publishing
Cebu, Philippines

Published by Tharsis Highlands Publishing
Cebu, Philippines
https://tharsishighlands.wordpress.com/books/

Amazon Print Edition
May 2019
ISBN: 9781099824418

EBook Editions
Amazon Kindle—2016, 2018
Smashwords—2016, 2018

Cover photos: Petr Kratochvil via publicdomainpictures.net.
Cover design by Rod Martin, Jr.
On the cover, the dry, cracked earth signifies desert-like conditions to be found on an ocean-covered planet that is too cold. The green life with dew signifies lush conditions to be found on an ocean-covered planet that is warm or even a little hot. Life thrives in warmth and dies in the cold.

Typography fonts
Headings: Rockwell Extra Bold
Running Heads: Rockwell
Text: Palatino Linotype

Dedicated to my loving wife, Juvy

"Climate is what on an average we may expect, weather is what we actually get" — *Andrew John Herbertson,* Outlines of Physiography, *circa 1901.*

Table of Contents

Introduction: Thermophobia in Perspective 1
Part 1: Thermophobia 17
Chapter 1: Unreasonable Fear 19
Chapter 2: The Current Ice Age..37
Chapter 3: Wonderful and Essential Carbon Dioxide 43
Chapter 4: 'Climate Change' and Other Squishy Terms 51
Chapter 5: The Missing Global Warming Catastrophes.................61
Chapter 6: The Bad Boys—IPCC, Climate Gate and Mr. Hockey
Stick 69
Chapter 7: Death of the African Dream; Death of the American
Dream 91
Chapter 8: The Real Culprit Behind Climate Change 99
Part 2: Cryophilia...107
Chapter 9: End of the Holocene..109
Chapter 10: Ninety Thousand Years of Ice 111
Chapter 11: Geoengineering 115
Chapter 12: Why? 121
Part 3: The Cure..129
Chapter 13: A Warm World 131
Chapter 14: Awareness of the Lies and the Real Problems...........135
Chapter 15: Prepare Humanity for the Cold (if necessary) 139
Chapter 16: End the Ice Age (if possible) 143
Chapter 17: Selflessness—Giving Up Self-Concern....................149
Appendix..153
References...155
Glossary 163

Videography 169
Links to Illustrations 173
About Rod Martin, Jr. 175
Other Books by Rod Martin, Jr. 177
Connect with Rod Martin, Jr. 183

Introduction: Thermophobia in Perspective

"One of the brightest gems in the New England weather is the dazzling uncertainty of it." —Mark Twain, speech to the New England Society, December 22, 1876

Thermophobia is a fear of warmth—a disease which has gripped much of the planet in recent years. Every fear about global warming will be cured in this book. We will use facts, logic, science and a sense of perspective that has been sorely missing from much of the mainstream media. Don't misunderstand this. Caring about the planet and our future is the foundation of this book.

Let us start with some simple questions.

Do you fear cuddling? Do you shake in terror over the idea of wrapping up in a warm blanket on a cold, rainy or snowy night? Does the notion of a warm bath or shower send chills up your spine? And do you stand frozen in horror thinking about sitting down to a nice, hot meal?

No?

Then why has civilization gone suddenly bonkers over a rise in average global temperature of 5.4 °F (3 °C) *over the next century?* That's a temperature difference some people would be hard pressed to discern. That's a yearly increase of only 0.06 °F (0.035 °C), barely enough to be measurable by most and felt by none. When a similar, natural rate of warming delivered us from the frozen horrors of the Little Ice Age, no one complained.

Let's do some comparison.

Downtown Los Angeles has a coastal, Mediterranean-type climate with an average daily high in the rainy month of February of 68.6 °F (20.3 °C) and an average daily low of 49.3 °F (9.6 °C). This gives us a daily range of about 19.3 °F (10.7 °C). *Frightening!* That's more than three times the dreaded increase foretold by the United Nations. But the people in Southern California don't seem to mind. And that's once a day, every day in February. And that's a minor fluctuation, dampened by the weather and proximity to the Pacific Ocean.

Phoenix, Arizona has an inland, high desert climate with an average daily high in dry June of 103.9 °F (39.9 °C) and an average daily low of 77.7 °F (25.4 °C). This gives us a daily range of a whopping 26.2 °F (14.5 °C). *Terrifying!* And yet Phoenix has been such a magnet, its population has grown from nearly 107,000 in 1950 to over 1.4 million in 2010—an increase of nearly 14 times. When my younger brother, Terry, worked for the US Postal Service, he told me they were opening up a new route or two every month just to keep up.

Over a twelve-month period, every year, temperatures in Los Angeles vary from an average low of 47.5 °F (8.6 °C) to an average high of 84.4 °F (29.1 °C). That's a *mind-numbing* yearly change of 36.9 °F (20.5 °C)—nearly seven times the UN's horror story.

For the yearly changes in Phoenix, we might just *blow a gasket*. Temperatures there vary from an average low of 44.8 °F (7.1 °C) to an average high of 106.1 °F (41.2 °C). That's a yearly change of 61.3 °F (34.1 °C)—every year, over eleven times the "global warming" scare story. People in Phoenix are not freaking out over this amount of yearly temperature change. Maybe they know something the UN doesn't.

Climate is a complex, non-linear system which is globally stable and locally unpredictable. This means that the entire planet will experience changes gradually. Simple inputs, however do not necessarily have simple outputs. Increase the water vapor worldwide, and you will tend to increase the potential rainfall overall, but the rainfall at any one location will remain unpredictable. But even that effect is not simple. Global warming will cause more evaporation from the oceans, but it will also result in the air being able to hold more water vapor before it precipitates as rain or snow. Non-linear simply means that the effects are displayed as curves on graphs rather than straight lines. Some of those curves can be quite complex.

Also, there are many things we do not yet know about the processes and effects within the climate and weather systems. We don't yet know the sensitivity of temperature change with changes in carbon dioxide. The paleoclimatic record tends to show that temperature has a relatively low sensitivity to changes in CO_2, but that's only a qualitative assessment. We don't yet know the exact quantity of this sensitivity. Thus, UN climate models will continue to yield outputs which do not match reality. Also, we do not yet know all of the factors which change climate. For instance, we're still studying the processes by which clouds are formed and their effect on overall climate.

More questions!

Where do most people want to vacation—snow or beach—cold climate or warm? Where do New Yorkers like to retire, if they have the money—Greenland or Florida? Which provides a more hospitable environment for growing crops—cold or warm? Where are we more likely to grow the food to feed millions—Antarctica or Java?

If you've been paying attention to the world around you, likely you will give the warmer answer for each of these questions. This seems to be almost a no-brainer, yet the news and government reports are awash with the horrors of global warming! Thus the ironic term, *thermophobia*—a fear of warmth.

In 2013, according to Mike Schneider of *Business Insider,* an estimated 537,000 residents moved to Florida and 10% of them were from New York state—or about 54,000. An estimated zero residents moved to Greenland. Certainly, real estate is far cheaper in Greenland, but facilities and infrastructure are largely nonexistent there. The infrastructure is missing, because the demand is near nonexistent. Warmer climates trump colder ones by a vast margin.

When we compare the population density of various latitudes, we see a clear correlation. Southern United States, including California, Oklahoma, Tennessee, North Carolina and states farther south, have an average density of 49.02 people per square kilometer. Northern states have an average population density of 28.48 people per square kilometer. Southern Canada has 6.82 people per square kilometer, while Northern Canada drops to 0.16 people per square kilometer. The gradation is clear. People like it warmer.

Below is a map showing the population gradient for the entire world by 10° latitude bands. This is based not on total population, but population per square kilometer of land for each band. Part of the reason for the bias toward the northern hemisphere has to do with the warming effect of the Gulf Stream. That flow of warmer water makes higher latitudes more livable in Europe than they would otherwise be.

In Canada, for instance, the southern border of Northwest Territories stands at 60°N. The closest large city to this latitude is Yellowknife with a population of about 19,000 people. Near that same latitude in Sweden is the capital city, Stockholm. Its metropolitan area has a population of over 2.1 million people. Oslo, Norway has about the same latitude and a metro area population of over 1.7 million.

0   10   20   30   40   50   60   70   80   90   100 110 120 130 140 150
People per square kilometer

The amount of warming being predicted as "catastrophic," most people would barely notice. The charts being bandied about by politicians and computer climate modelers show mountains of temperature increase that really are only fractions of a single degree. We're looking at mountains that are visible only under a microscope. The error bars of data sometimes are nearly as large as the swings in the data. In other words, someone is making a big deal out of practically nothing.

In the 1970s, after three decades of global cooling, newspapers and magazines ran the scare headlines that we might be entering a new Ice Age.

Okay, now hold onto your hats for a moment. We're already in an Ice Age. That "thing" that supposedly ended 11,500–17,000 years ago was called the most recent "glacial period" of the *current Ice Age*—a period of global cold that has been going on for the last 2.6 million years.

Yes, we are in an Ice Age. You know those "little" white things on the poles of the planet? Whenever those persist throughout the year, we're in an Ice Age, and they have done that for more than two million years.

If you look at a chart of the last 500 million years, you'll see that our "dangerous" warming trend has not yet pulled us out of the trough of cold which Earth entered nearly three million years ago.

When NASA, the news media, and motion pictures characterize Earth's warming trend as a "fever," they are being dishonest. If they were selling a product with those lies, they would be guilty of criminal fraud. Earth has been cold for nearly three million years. We have experienced a brief thaw called the Holocene. If you are starting to understand the implications of this, you should join us in wishing that the thaw continues. After all, global warming 12,000 years ago made civilization possible by increasing rain, decreasing violent storms and shrinking the sizes of deserts. Life blossomed because of that warming.

Understand this: Climate has always changed and always will, with or without humans. Every change will bring its share of problems. Warmth, it seems, brings far fewer problems than cold. A 2014 CDC report by J. Berko and D. Ingram, *et al,* shows that deaths from cold (6,660) are near exactly twice as prevalent as deaths from heat (3,332). Their statistics covered the period 2006–2010. But this is only a small part of the larger climate picture.

The Holocene "Warm" Period

The Holocene—that period of geological time which began about 11,500–17,000 years ago—is the current interglacial (between glacial periods) of the current Ice Age. It's somewhat warmer than the glacial periods, but it's still Ice Age material. Regrettably, interglacials have a nasty habit of ending. They typically last about 11,000 years, on average, so we're overdue for a return to glacial conditions. It could happen later today. Or it might be several thousand years before the Holocene bids us *adieu*.

Of the last nine interglacials, the duration ranged from 4,000 to 28,000 years. The 28,000-year duration was right after an exceedingly long glacial of 143,000 years. So, there is a broad range of duration variability. Also, there is a broad range of warmth experienced during interglacials. The most recent interglacial—the Eemian—was as much as 5 °C warmer than our current "scary" temperature. This likely melted all the Arctic sea ice and polar bears survived just fine.

Quite often, it takes an interglacial several hundred years to end, but they have ended as quickly as 50 years. If the Holocene end were to start tomorrow with a 50-year schedule, your grandchildren would likely see permanent snow in the northern and mid-latitude states of America. The corn and wheat belts would suffer from permanent cold. Crops would fail. Welcome to 90,000 years of frozen wasteland. Canadians would have to move to the United States. Many Americans may be forced to move to Mexico. There's a switch for you.

Global Warming is Good

With all the bad things being said about global warming these days, this may seem to be a shocking statement for some. Nearly every bad thing said against global warming is slander—a lie. When you are finished with this book, this point will be abundantly clear to you. But if you remain in doubt, I recommend that you check the facts behind each claim. Realize that some sources are quite willing to lie, so don't depend on only one source or group of sources.

As this book was in the final stages of preparation for release, I encountered two separate individuals who were quite passionate in their disbelief that global warming could be good. Their concern was very real to them, but based on misconceptions. They felt that warming the planet would cause some areas to burn up, destroying people and the local ecology. And they were so passionate about their beliefs that they could not hear any evidence disproving that danger.

If you believe as they do, but you remain one of those rare individuals who can learn new things, then read on. If not, then you are not yet ready for this book. It's not for you.

All changes come with their own set of problems. Sometimes, we need to chose a path which comes with fewer extreme problems. This is at the heart of the climate debate.

Earth won't burn up from even a 20 °C of warming. Why? Earth has a temperature regulator. It's called water. The liquid oceans of the Earth have kept the global average temperature from changing more than 5% throughout the measurable climate history of our world—more than three billion years. That's amazingly steady for such a chaotic, non-linear system.

How does it work? When things warm up, the oceans evaporate more water which cools things off. And all that extra water vapor forms more clouds which cool down the planet even further with some nice shade.

So, NASA calling our minor thaw a "fever" is not only inaccurate (not scientific), it's downright political and an appeal to emotion (anti-science).

Water also helps on the cooling side, too. Water resists temperature change. It takes a great deal of energy, or lack of it, to change the temperature of the oceans. If the air cools off, the warmer oceans help to restore some of the lost warmth. Coastal regions are the most protected. Inland deserts don't benefit as much and that's why their daily temperatures fluctuate the most of any region.

Ice floats and protects deeper water from easy freezing. If frozen water were to sink, the bottoms of the oceans would likely never thaw.

When oceans cool, there is less evaporation, so less cooling. Because there's less water vapor in the air, there are fewer clouds to shade the world. Both of these effects promote greater warmth to protect us from runaway cooling.

This one molecule—so vital to life—is also vital to maintaining a habitable planet.

Sea level rise is the only significant global warming danger, but it's slow moving. People and ecosystems can move. Moving is far easier than dying from the many dangers caused by global cooling.

Caring for the Planet is a Good Thing

Most any rational human being would want their home planet to be safe for their families and friends. We want an end to pollution, wars, excessive greed and corporate callousness. But someone has tapped into this powerful human motivation and redirected it toward evil. Ooo-oo-oh, yes—evil. If warmth is good and someone is demonizing warmth, they are either insane or psychopathic. I'm not sure which is worse.

When Al Gore's famous documentary came out, I was an immediate fan. Why? Because I care about our planet. That was the main thrust of the film. Also, it had the word "truth" in the title. I should have known better that liars like calling their statements "truth."

Carbon dioxide happens to be an essential gas of life— and not a pollutant. But it's being treated as pollution. We hear the term "carbon pollution." We hear of the "carbon" problem as if it were "soot," instead of a clear, odorless and vital gas of life. At the beginning of the Industrial Revolution, CO_2 was supposedly at about 280ppm (parts-per-million). That's not very much. In fact, if CO_2 levels were half of that, all plant life would start to die; and then all animal life would die from the growing lack of oxygen (formerly produced by plants). And, without plants for food, all animal life would die. Today's current level is about 400ppm.

Over the last 500 million years, CO_2 levels have rarely been this low. During a significant percentage of that period, carbon dioxide levels were at or above 1,000ppm, sometimes staying above 2,000ppm for millions of years. One long stretch during the Cretaceous enjoyed 4,000ppm of carbon dioxide.

The space station has CO_2 levels set at 5,000ppm for optimum operation. Navy submarines use 8,000ppm—nearly 20 times the current atmospheric level.

If we truly cared about our planet, we would increase CO_2 levels to about 1,000ppm and increase warmth, too. Let us end the Ice Age, before it kills billions of us when the Holocene ends.

Ironically, some people think corporations are evil, but believe the corporate news media on climate. Some people think a degree of cooling would be equally as disruptive as an equivalent amount of warming. But they are living in a delusion, because they don't know the dangers of ice and are ignoring the benefits of warmth.

In our own history, the world has suffered greatly from the cooling effects of one volcanic eruption. In 1816, Earth experienced a Year Without Summer. There were massive famines. Thousands died. Thousands more became climate refugees. And this was a minor cold event compared to a glacial period of the current Ice Age. Yet, CIA Director John Brennan, on June 29, 2016, gave a talk at the Council on Foreign Relations to say wonderful things about cooling the planet with particles strewn in the upper atmosphere like the volcanoes of the past. As CIA director, I suspect he's not entirely ignorant. That would seem to make him a genocidal psychopath, instead.

So, who would be making us fear warmth? Clearly, someone who is either ignorant or doesn't mind lying on a truly large scale. I had one concerned citizen tell me that a lie about climate was okay so long as it motivated people to stop polluting the planet. But conflating healthy, helpful CO_2 and global warming with toxic pollution is misguided at best. And disrupting the global economy by making energy too expensive would not necessarily achieve the clean environment most of us desire. Corporations break the law all the time. Even when they are caught, taken to court and prosecuted, they pay small fines compared to their huge profits. To them, criminal activity is profitable.

Conspiracy?

If you think no one would ever commit such a planet-wide conspiracy, think again. Conspiracies are extremely common, because people are selfish or self-concerned. Every war started with at least one conspiracy. Every drug deal. Every multi-perpetrator crime. In fact, in my book, *Dirt Ordinary: Shining a Light on Conspiracies*, I show that there are at least 489 new conspiracies starting each second, somewhere in the world, day-in and day-out, all year long, and every year. That's more than 29,000 new conspiracies starting each minute, more than 1.7 million new conspiracies starting each hour, and more than 42 million new conspiracies starting every day. You get the idea—as ordinary as dirt.

Do you think for a minute that someone with tens of billions of dollars doesn't lust for a few trillion? This boggles the mind for most people. How can any one individual have tens of billions of dollars. And if a petty thug could kill you for pocket change, do you think for a minute that rich psychopaths would not stop with killing thousands or millions to gain more power?

Is there a conspiracy going on, or is this madness merely the product of collective foolishness and blindness? Whatever the truth behind it all, don't let a knee-jerk aversion to "conspiracy talk" blind you to what might actually be going on. The smart human is the aware human.

Confession of a Bias

I have to confess that I have a bias against warmer temperatures. I like my air-conditioning. I prefer a cool breeze to a warm one, all other things being equal. I grew up in semi-arid West Texas, suffering the hot southern sun throughout grade school. So, why would I move to Phoenix, Arizona and live there for ten years? Why would I then move to the tropics, currently having lived in the Philippines for more than eight years?

The full answers are not simple. But some things are far more important than temperature. My move in 1997 from Los Angeles to Phoenix was job-related. The first two summers there, I felt like I was melting or roasting. My move in 2007 from Phoenix to the Philippines was love-related. The heat plus humidity were occasionally unbearable, but I survived. I'm still biased against warmer weather, and love the cooler, rainy season and the colder, provincial interior, but I've acclimated quite nicely.

Despite this bias against warmth, I wholeheartedly support Global Warming, because it promotes life and may help save all of us and civilization, too. I do not work for, and I am not in any way compensated by any corporation for my views on climate (not yet, anyway). I don't get paid by "big oil," though I have to admit that my late father once worked for Humble Oil Company (now a part of Exxon), but that was more than half a century ago.

What's Ahead?

In **Part 1, Thermophobia,** we look at,

(1) **Unreasonable Fear** (paranoia). In this book, we will be looking at several "climate change" lies and the facts that set them straight. We start out by facing our fears and separating the truly troublesome from the far larger array of inconsequential facts.

(2) **The Current Ice Age.** We will look at the fact that Global Warming is good. There's so much common sense packed into this chapter, that you'll be amazed that so many have never seen through the Madison Avenue sales job being done on them.

(3) **Wonderful and Essential Carbon Dioxide.** Carbon dioxide gets a clean slate, because it's also very good for life. We'll look at the facts and the hype, digging deeper into the controversy than you may ever have been. It'll be a quick look, but an important one. We also look at the economics of Carbon Tax and the Carbon Footprint fraud.

(4) **'Climate Change' and Other Squishy Terms.** Don't be confused by the term "climate change," either. Someone is messing with our language, like calling "war" a "peace-keeping action." Climate has always changed. It can't help but change. That's natural. But in today's deceitful dialog, the term "climate change" has been kidnapped and made to wear a frightful mask. Our lovely child now looks like a demon.

Then, we focus on the state of science. We will see how science, peer review and research funding have all become corrupted.

If you've followed the "climate change" story, at all, you likely know that Big Oil is behind the "climate change" deniers. Well, hold onto your hat (again). Big Oil has contributed to both sides of this debate. Why would they do that? We will look at some obvious possibilities.

(5) **The Missing Global Warming Catastrophes.** On the catastrophe front, we will look at the real facts about what is happening to hurricanes-typhoons, tornadoes, droughts and floods. Nothing out of the ordinary! In fact, many catastrophes have been on a decline. The news says one thing, but reality says another.

(6) **The Bad Boys—IPCC, Climate-Gate and Mr. Hockey Stick.** We will look at the IPCC (Intergovernmental Panel on Climate Change), the Climate-Gate fraud and how governments have whitewashed their sickly step-child and given it a clean bill of health.

(7) **Death of the African Dream; Death of the American Dream.** And then we take a look at the struggling Third World and what all this "carbon" hysteria is doing to their dream of development. But along with Africa, America's corrupt government is betraying its own industries to shut them down and destroy the nation's economy. Why would an

American president and Congress do such a thing? The answers are far bigger than climate change.

(8) **The Real Culprit Behind Climate Change.** Just as CO_2 levels are tiny compared to nitrogen, oxygen and water vapor levels, Earth is extremely tiny compared to its largest source of energy—the sun.

Part 2: Cryophilia, includes,

(9) **End of the Holocene.** When our current interglacial warm period of the current Ice Age, ends, we will, more than likely, be returned to glacial conditions that will kill off most of Earth's population.

(10) **Ninety Thousand Years of Ice.** This is what we have to look forward to.

(11) **Geoengineering.** Though the scientists claim they're only talking about implementing geoengineering, in actual fact they've been doing it for years and ridiculing anyone who notices it. It's very much like the Emperor's New Clothes. The imperial officials ridicule people for noticing the nakedness. Hilarious, but also dangerous. Geoengineering to cool the planet in the midst of an Ice Age is like sewing a hungry man's mouth shut. Dumb. Criminal!

(12) **Why?** Why would anyone go to all this trouble to spread such a huge lie? What is their hidden agenda?

Part 3: The Cure, includes,

(13) **A Warm World.** Imagine a world without polar ice.

(14) Awareness of the Lies and the Real Problems. You can't solve a problem if you're not first aware of it.

(15) **Prepare Humanity for the Cold (if necessary).** If we have to, we need to figure out how we're going to feed 7+ Billion people when most of the farm land is under several feet of snow all year long.

(16) **End the Ice Age (if possible).** What if human ingenuity was good enough to fix this climate problem once

and for all? I doubt if we can get it done by governments or corporations as the driving force.

(17) **Selflessness—Giving Up Self-Concern.** I think we need a new force on the block—a force called love—the real kind of love that doesn't need anything in return. This may seem naive to some, but consider this wisdom: We cannot cure darkness with more darkness. We cannot cure hate with more hate. All of the evil of this world comes back to self-concern (ego); and we cannot cure self-concern with more self-concern. The opposite of self-concern is altruistic, unconditional love. When we give up self-concern, we ironically gain infinite potential.

Note: Originals of the pictures used in this book may be found using the links in the "Links to Illustrations" section in the Appendix. If any links no longer work, try archive.org to retrieve a snapshot of the file from the past.

Remember this key idea: life thrives in the warmth and dies in the cold.

I'm your fellow citizen on this planet. I want to know what you think. But more than that, I want you to survive and thrive.

Rod Martin, Jr.
July, 7, 2016
Cebu, Philippines

Part 1: Thermophobia

thermophobia *n.*—An abnormal fear of warmth or heat (*thermo-*, related to, caused by, or measuring heat or warmth; -*phobia*, an intense fear of or aversion to a specified thing)

Chapter 1: Unreasonable Fear

"When the wise man points at the moon, the fool looks at the finger." —Attributed to be a Chinese proverb

What you don't know about global warming could kill you. The only problem is, the United Nations, NASA and so many other corrupt bodies have it upside-down and backwards. Listening to them will pollute your mind.

It may sound ludicrous to say that the world is wrong and little old me is right. But let us use the facts, rather than popularity or authority to rule our judgment. As you will learn, it's not the "world" in opposition to this work. No, it's a far, far smaller portion who lie about their numbers. To them, perception is everything, and if you perceive only the lie, then that lie becomes your reality. Four years ago, that was me.

First of all, an unreasonable fear, not based upon facts, is typically called *paranoia*. This is a byproduct of the current epidemic of thermophobia. Fear of warmth is a manufactured fear. As we all know, no one in their right mind fears cuddling with a healthy loved one. No one is terrified of a warm shower or a hot meal.

These days, when something bad happens in the weather, the mainstream news media points to global warming as the cause. Heat wave: global warming. Cold snap: global warming. Hurricanes and tornadoes: global warming. Drought: global warming. Flood: global warming. Economic upheaval: global warming. Election lost to the Democrats: global warming. Election lost to the Republicans: global warming. And since global warming took a holiday after 1998, simply replace the term with "climate change," but keep the Carbon Tax, because we need to reduce the global warming which no longer exists. Confused? Could this be by design?

The problem is, they've come up with short, but inaccurate terms that are misleading. By "global warming," they mean "man made catastrophic global warming." But the ironic thing is, there is very little truth in what they say. They confuse real damage from chemical pollution with fictional damage from warming and CO_2. Nearly all of the disasters about which they wring their hands are false. By the time you're finished with this book, you will understand *why* they are false.

An Inconvenient Lie—Al Gore's Contribution to Hysteria

In 2006, former vice president of the United States, Al Gore, came out with a film called, *An Inconvenient Truth*. I was an instant fan. I like the idea of people taking responsibility and helping to save the planet from the dangers of pollution and other, harmful human activities.

Gore's film had a lot going for it. First of all, it had "truth" in the title. Second, it was a slick production with good writing and excellent graphics. Third, it had a smooth-talking politician delivering the message. But perhaps the most important aspect was that it talked about caring for the planet. That hit home. That one point connected viscerally and deeply.

But the film was a sham.

In the midst of the film, Gore had a huge graph of temperature and carbon dioxide (CO_2) levels behind him. He made a big deal about a vividly apparent correlation between the rising and falling of both graphs. On a scale of a few hundred thousand years, the correlation seemed undeniable. There were only minor differences, but the broad swath of increases and decreases were in lock-step, like a mirror image.

But let's think about this carefully. What can cause increased CO_2 back 500,000 years ago? Certainly not human civilization. According to today's anthropologists, humans didn't come on the scene until 200,000 years ago. Gore's film implies that CO_2 came first and caused global temperatures to rise. Yet, he and his fellow global warming alarmists cannot tell us where the extra CO_2 came from.

The first principle of causality requires that the cause must come before the effect.

Here's a simple example. You cannot plant a seed before the fruit from which the seed is derived has grown. No fruit, no seed. Another example: A man cannot drive a car before it is manufactured. See?

The problem with Al Gore's correlated graphs is that the temperature rises first. The CO_2 rises roughly 800 years later. And scientists know why. The oceans store many million tons of carbon dioxide. Warming the oceans forces the CO_2 out. But water resists warming. It takes a great deal of energy to warm up that much water—800 years of energy. Could it be that a large part of the CO_2 increases we're now experiencing are from ocean warming after the Little Ice Age ended nearly 200 years ago? We don't know, but it's plausible.

On Gore's huge stage graph, 800 years was barely a sliver. If Gore's graph was 30 feet long, then 800 years would be half an inch wide. Because the two graphs were separated—one above the other—it would prove difficult for any audience to see which graph led the other. Clever sleight-of-hand. Was that a mere accident or intentional misdirection?

Some proponents of the global warming scare tell us that carbon dioxide released from the oceans later increased the temperature even more. Yes, but how much. If increased CO_2 creates a series of runaway positive feedbacks, then how did the Earth ever cool down while the atmosphere had 2,000ppm (parts-per-million) or even 4,000ppm of CO_2? Near the Ordovician-Silurian boundary, temperatures plummeted to one of the lowest ever on Earth, yet the CO_2 content seems to have been well over 2,000ppm.

We need to point out that paleoclimatic measurements tend to vary as new data is gathered and refinements are made. The best we can say is that there remains a great deal we do not yet know about climate changes. In other words, the science is definitely not settled. Anyone who tries to sell you the idea that science is settled, either doesn't know how science works or they are attempting to hide something.

It's a Catastrophe!

Gore's film portrayed greenhouse gases as thugs which beat up on poor Mr. Sunbeam and trapped him on Earth. Because of this, poor polar bears don't have as much ice to climb onto.

During the far warmer Holocene Optimum, polar bears may well have had zero ice onto which to climb, yet they thrived. Life thrives in the warmth. Even penguins in Ant-arctica have to keep their eggs warm so they'll hatch. The cold would kill them. Polar bear numbers have climbed steadily because of the warmth. Warmer climate means more food to feed their babies. And polar bears are strong swimmers who do not need ice. Photographers find polar bears climbing on ice so that the ursine creatures can get a better look at what may be a potential food source—the photographer and the ship from which they are taking their photos. Ice, rock, tree stump—it doesn't matter to the bear. Gore's film made it seem that ice was essential to the bears' survival, but that was an outright lie.

Gore makes many blunders in his film. At about 46 minutes he says that "Earth's climate is a non-linear system" which he says is a "fancy" way of "saying that the changes are not all just gradual. Some of them come suddenly." His definition is wrong! Non-linearity merely means it's a curved graph. You can have a linear relationship which is extremely steep and sudden. You can have a non-linear relationship which is gradual. Things like Gore's incorrect definition make his film junk science.

He says that the average annual temperature of the Earth is 58 °F. He says that if we have an increase of 5 °F, which is on the low end of the projections, that's only +1° F at the equator, but +12° F at the poles. This sounds about right, but where Gore gets it wrong has to do with storms and their energy. If both the poles and the equator had nearly the same temperature, as they seem to be on Venus, then there would be very little energy for storms. You don't get violent storms from heat; you get them from a temperature difference—like voltage potential in a battery. If both terminals of a battery are +300 volts, then you have no energy output. But if one is +1 volt and the other is −1 volt, then you get a nice current flowing, because there is a difference of 2 volts. Making the polar temperatures closer to that of the equator makes storms less likely and less energetic, because there is less temperature difference.

At about 28 minutes into his film, Al Gore talks about another graph that shows temperature since the American Civil War. What he fails to point out is that there are repetitive cycles of down and up trends and the most recent is merely a repetition of the former trends—natural and not man made. During World War II, industry went crazy building up for war. That's a big surge in CO_2 output. After the war, we had a post-war boom that made industrial output of CO_2 skyrocket. Yet, during all that time, from the start of World War II, global temperatures were going down. Suddenly, the correlation between CO_2 and temperature falls apart. Did Gore stop and explain why? Of course not. He had a catastrophe to sell. He could not be bothered with little details like a lack of correlation between carbon dioxide and temperature. He couldn't be concerned with something as important as the real truth.

Here's a graph of a similar period. Notice the roughly 30-year trends based on a 60-year cycle. This cycle started before our 20th century industrialization and massive CO_2 output. Was it purely natural? Notice how the trend from 1910 to 1940 is very similar to the terrifying trend from 1970 to 2000.

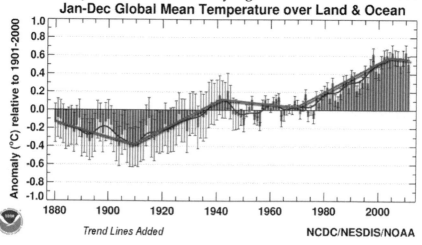

Jan-Dec Global Mean Temperature over Land & Ocean

Trend Lines Added   NCDC/NESDIS/NOAA

About one-third of the way through his documentary, Mr. Gore claims that the United States set an all-time record for number of tornadoes in 2004—"New record for tornados — 1,717." On a chart of EF-1 and stronger tornadoes produced from data by NOAA, the year 2004 had only 600 tornadoes. If Gore's data is accurate, then this means that 1,117 tornadoes were weaker than EF-1. Greater population density and more sophisticated techniques of tornado detection are helping to increase the number of tornadoes reported. This, by itself, is not necessarily a product of any climate change; it's very likely a product of better technology and more people available to report on the weaker tornadoes. I've seen many "dust devils" or mini-tornadoes when I lived in West Texas and I never reported a one of them. Each one lasted perhaps a few seconds or up to a minute.

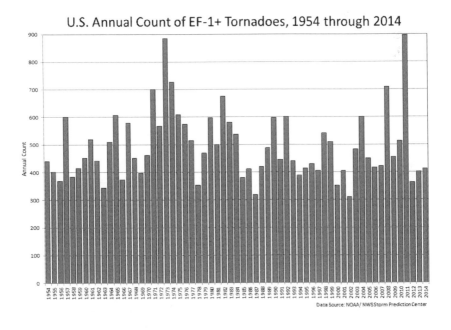

U.S. Annual Count of EF-1+ Tornadoes, 1954 through 2014

Data Source: NOAA/ NWS Storm Prediction Center

On the same NOAA (National Oceanographic and Atmospheric Administration) chart where 2004 was supposedly a record setter for all tornadoes, no matter how weak, we have 1957, 1980, 1990 and 1992 which were close to the same for the number of stronger tornadoes. But 1965 and 1975 were slightly higher in count, while 1971 had about 700, 1973 had about 890, 1974 had about 720, and 1982 had about 680. Overall, the trend in EF-1 and stronger tornadoes has remained relatively flat, with lots of ups and downs around the mean.

When you look at NOAA's data for the same period, but for the strongest tornadoes—EF-3 to EF-5—there is a definite, sixty-year *down* trend. Only about 28 strong tornadoes in 2004, compared to 68 in 1982, 87 in 1973, 102 in 1965 and 137 in 1974. In the 2000s, the highest three counts of strong tornadoes were 44 in 2010, 59 in 2008 and 83 in 2011. The years 2012–2014 were all under 30 strong tornadoes each year.

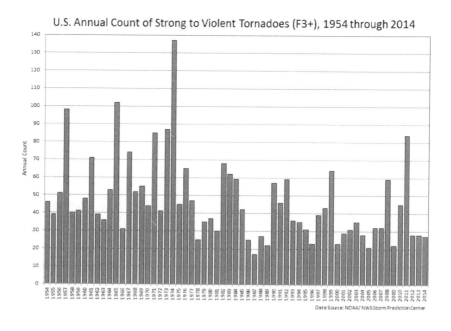

U.S. Annual Count of Strong to Violent Tornadoes (F3+), 1954 through 2014

Data Source: NOAA/ NWS Storm Prediction Center

So, the scare is empty.

Any change in climate can cause problems. We deal with them when they come. We put on our "hat" of compassion and help out. Warming would be a catastrophe if we had enough heat to boil the oceans away, but that would require an increase of 85.6 °C—from 14.4 °C to 100 °C. The United Nations is talking about a 3 °C increase, not 85 °C. We're talking about melting ice, not boiling the oceans. We're talking about getting warm, instead of freezing.

When Gore talked about Katrina, he forgot to mention that New Orleans had begged for federal help strengthening its levees, but received far less than that for which they had asked. The state of Louisiana had asked for "$27.1 million for shoring up levees," according to Michael Grunwald of the Washington Post, but "Bush suggested $3.9 million, and Congress agreed to spend $5.7 million." Grunwald added, though, "Lt. Gen. Carl Strock, the chief of the Corps, has said that in any event, more money would not have prevented the drowning of the city, since its levees were designed to protect against a Category 3 storm, and the levees that failed were already completed projects."

Perhaps it was wrong for them to assume that New Orleans would never receive a category 5 hurricane. Perhaps it was wrong to have a city so close to the sea and up to six and a half feet below sea level. Half measures in a potentially dangerous situation are a recipe for disaster.

Will Bunch, in his article for Alternet.org, portrayed a slightly different picture of the Louisiana problem. He said that the federal government was diverting funds toward the burgeoning War in Iraq and toward the build-up of the new Department of Homeland Security. The Bush White House lied about weapons of mass destruction in Iraq, so the diversion of funds was based upon less than honorable pretenses. They attacked Afghanistan, despite the Afghani willingness to turn over Osama Bin Laden only if the Americans could turn over proof of Bin Laden's complicity. But either America had no proof, or they preferred war. I don't know which is more infuriating and scary. Perhaps we have to reassess the all-too-common desire to build homes and cities next to oceans, to avoid taking responsibility for proper upkeep and the priorities of what appears to have been a corrupt government.

We will look more closely at extreme weather events in a later chapter.

When Gore talks about the oceanic conveyor belt, or thermohaline (temperature-salt) circulation, he says that the sudden flush of cold, fresh water from the North American glaciation shut off the oceans' conveyor belt, creating a freshwater cap that plunged Europe back into another Ice Age. What Mr. Gore seems ignorant of is that the Ice Age didn't end or restart. We're still in an Ice Age. What ended and restarted were the glacial conditions of a cold, glacial period. Scientists call that 1300-year period of renewed cold, the "Younger Dryas" or "Big Freeze." After thousands of years of thawing, Earth's climate had taken three steps backward. Gore said the return to Ice Age conditions took as little as ten years. From all I've read, scientists suspect it took as little as fifty, but Gore is a salesman or politician. Exaggeration is to be expected.

He suggests that melting Greenland could shut down the modern thermohaline circulation. This is certainly something to keep in mind, but the Greenland glacier is far smaller than the North American glacier was at the beginning of the Younger Dryas. According to Paterson, "Volume estimates for the Laurentide ice sheet are 26.5 x 106 km3 at maximum [~24,500 BC], 17.5 x 106 km3 at 11,800 B.P. [9,850 BC]." According to the National Snow & Ice Data Center (NSIDC), Antarctica contains about ten times as much ice as does Greenland. They estimate that Antarctica contains some 30 million cubic kilometers of ice. This means that Greenland must possess roughly 3 million cubic kilometers. If we take the Laurentide (North American) ice sheet volume to have been 18 million cubic kilometers at the beginning of the Younger Dryas (10,900 BC), then it would have contained six times as much ice as Greenland does today.

Gore blames the modern rates of species extinctions on global warming. He forgets that humans are polluting the environment with heavy metal toxins, harsh petrochemical sludge, plastic islands in the oceans and scientific mon-strosities like GMOs dowsed with greater and greater quantities of poisonous herbicides, like Roundup. So, how many species are dying because they are being poisoned, compared to those which are unable to move to a different climatic zone?

What's ironic about Monsanto's rush to put genetically modified organisms into the world-at-large, is that the gov-ernment agency depended on the company's meager 3-month safety test. That's like a major airline manufacturer coming up with a radically new airplane design and testing it for 15 minutes before lining up the paying public. The customers are becoming the guinea pigs!

Gore talked about "a collision between our civilization and the earth." He talked of three factors:

- Population (food demand, water demand, natural resource demand)
- Science and technology (old habits + old tech = predictable consequences)
- Our way of thinking (boiling frog syndrome)

Gore's film claims, "Number disagreeing with the global consensus that greenhouse gas pollution has caused most of the warming of the last 50 years: 0..." based on peer reviewed articles of the last ten years. But his claim that there is no disagreement with his thesis is wrong. Here is a list of a few of the climate scientists who disagree quite vocally:

- Dr. David Legates, Center for Climatic Research, University of Delaware.
- Jorgen Peder Steffensen, curator, Niels Bohr Institute, Dept. of Geophysics.
- Dr. John Christy, University of Alabama in Huntsville (former IPCC lead author).
- Dr. Nils-Axel Morner, former head of the paleogeophysics and geodynamics department at Stockholm University.
- Professor Tim Ball, Dept. of Climatology, University of Winnipeg.
- Professor Ian Clark, Dept. of Earth Sciences, University of Ottawa.
- Professor Richard Lindzen, IPCC & MIT.
- Professor Philip Stott, Dept. of Biogeography, University of London.
- Professor Syun-Ichi Akasofu, Director, International Arctic Research Centre.
- Dr. Piers Corbyn, Climate Forecaster, Weather Action.
- Professor Frederick Singer, former director, US National Weather Service.
- Dr. Roy Spencer, Weather Satellite Team Leader, NASA.
- Professor Patrick Michaels, Dept. of Environmental Sciences, University of Virginia, former IPCC author.
- Dr. Judith Curry, climatologist and former chair of the School of Earth and Atmospheric Sciences, Georgia Institute of Technology.

We have no idea how many scientists are merely going along with the "climate change" hoax in order to keep their sources of funding happy. That number could be huge. Scientists are people, after all, and people tend to remain self-concerned. To some, losing a job is more dangerous than bad science.

Gore makes an impassioned plea that scientists have been ridiculed and persecuted for thinking that global warming was a problem. But now that seems to have reversed. Some politicians are demanding the "deniers" be arrested. Scientists are losing their jobs or remaining quiet so they don't rock the "climate change" boat. Neither side of a debate should receive this kind of treatment.

Using an infographic supposedly produced by the political opposition in the administration of Bush, Sr., Gore pointed out that the image represented a false choice— between gold bars and the entire Earth. But one other false implication is Gore's message that doing things his way will save the entire planet. Arguably, this is the message of his entire documentary. This, then, becomes a double-layered falsehood. A lie wrapped around a false choice.

Gore said one very profound and wise thing—that doing the right thing will add to our prosperity and create lots of new jobs. But what is that "right thing?" That's what this book is about, in part.

The right thing is not crippling industry, taxing carbon dioxide output and shackling nations to an unelected, international body. The United Nations wants individual nations to give up some of their national sovereignty to an unelected body of climate police. They want that bureaucracy to have total power over climate issues and no exit clause. In other words, they want all nations to be trapped forever, even if the climate bureaucracy is later found to be corrupt. Whoever signs such a contract is not being very logical or ethical.

Gore said some profound things in his film. Politicians usually do. He let us all know that the pale blue dot known as Earth—our home—is at stake. That may be true, but jumping off of a cliff is the wrong direction to go. Jumping from much-needed warmth back into the freezer is lunacy, at best, and wholesale suicide, at its worst.

Gore's Film Contains Errors, Declares British Judge

UK reporter, David Adam, writing for *The Guardian*, let the world know that a high court judge—Mr. Justice Burton—had criticized the Oscar and Nobel prize winning film as flawed and that it contained what the judge characterized as nine significant errors. (Additional notes added that were not part of the article or judge's decision.)

- Gore's film declared that populated, low-lying Pacific atolls "are being inundated because of anthropogenic global warming." The problem is, none of them are being evacuated.

    Note: In fact, the Maldives, cited as one of the endangered nations, has shown signs that sea level has fallen. Professor Nils-Axel Mörner had visited the islands to investigate the claims of rising oceans. When he returned with a film crew, he had wanted to show them a lonely tree which seemed to defy the rising sea level hypothesis. When he found the tree laying on its side, he felt that he had been wrong. He asked the locals when the sea had taken the tree. They told him, "No," and that it had been a couple of Australian climate scientists who had pulled the tree down by hand. What motivated climate scientists to destroy property in a foreign country? Were they threatened by the implications to their "climate change" theory?

- The film talked about global warming "shutting down the ocean conveyor"—the method by which warm gulf stream water is moved from the Caribbean to western Europe. The judge said that, according to the IPCC, it was "very unlikely" that the ocean conveyor would stop in the future, but that it could slow down.

- In Gore's film, he had displayed two graphs, one plotting the temperature changes and the other fluctuations in CO_2 during the last 650,000 years. Gore had remarked that it showed "an exact fit." Even though scientists agree there is a link, "the two graphs do not establish what Mr. Gore asserts."

Note: Other scientists later noted that temperature increases led carbon dioxide increases by about 800 years, because the extra CO_2 came from dissolved gas in the oceans forced out by the warming ocean water. Gore had claimed carbon dioxide had caused the warming, but actually it was the other way around.

- Mr. Gore claimed that the loss of snow on Africa's Mt. Kilimanjaro was clearly attributable to human-caused climate change. The judge disagreed, stating that such a link had not been established.
- The film used the desiccation of the Sahel's Lake Chad as an example of global warming. The judge said, "It is apparently considered to be more likely to result from ... population increase, over-grazing and regional climate variability."
- Mr. Gore also attributed Hurricane Katrina to global warming, but there was "insufficient evidence to show that."
- In the film, Mr. Gore claimed that polar bears were being found that had drowned "swimming long distances to find the ice." The judge said, "The only scientific study that either side before me can find is one which indicates that four polar bears have recently been found drowned because of a storm."

Note: Polar bears have been found to be extremely powerful swimmers which can swim dozens of kilometers. Ice is not needed. Also, polar bear populations have been on the rise with the warming. This should not be surprising. These bears have thrived through at least two far warmer periods— Holocene Optimum (~4 °C warmer) and Eemian interglacial (~5 °C warmer).

- Gore's film argued that global warming and other factors were bleaching coral reefs all over the world. The judge pointed out that other factors, such as over-fishing, and pollution, could not be easily separated from the impacts of climate change.

- The judge ruled as "distinctly alarmist" the film's claim that a sea-level rise of up to 20 feet would be caused by melting of either west Antarctica or Greenland in the near future.

Note: With the findings of Nils-Axel Mörner, sea levels may have been falling in recent years. Some of the anecdotal reports of rising sea level may instead have been lowering land, as in the case of London and Southern England. That part of Great Britain is still suffering the slower after effects of post-glacial isostatic adjustment after the glacier melt over twelve thousand years ago. Those lands which were buried under ice are still rising. Nearby lands, like Chicago, on the southern shore of Lake Michigan, are still being sucked downward to compensate for the lands which are still rising.

Fear of Overpopulation

Besides fear of the climate, people are being manipulated by a fear that there are too many people using up our precious resources.

Population is not a problem. Overpopulation is not happening. What we're really seeing is mismanagement and the products of greed and insensitivity.

Birth rates are going down where societies reach prosperity. In fact, some countries have negative growth rates. Population seems to be self-stabilizing. The real problem is the suppression of peoples who are trying to lift themselves out of poverty. Globalists and their corporations care far more about profits than they do for the people who live in the nations from which they are draining the natural resources. If a claim that overpopulation is a problem ever could be made, it might be that the planet has entirely too many corporations. Would even one be too many?

I was curious how many people Earth could support with unselfish management. Logistics are always a concern, but say for the moment that everyone either lived in the mountains or on the ocean—on floating cities, or upon piers built atop sea mounts and continental shelves. If we used all of the flat land for growing crops, how many people could Earth support? We'll home in on an answer in just a moment. First however, let's take a closer look at our current population—about 7.5 billion.

One study showed that everyone could live in a plot of land the size of Texas with a 66 feet by 66 feet area for each family of four. That's a small human footprint for all of Mankind. Another study showed that all 7+ billion humans could fit inside the limits of New York City, if we removed all the buildings, trees and such. Shoulder-to-shoulder, that might be a little uncomfortable after the first few minutes. But this merely gives you an idea of scale.

An enterprising farmer found that he could create a million pounds of food every year on 3 acres of land, including 10,000 fish. He goes by the handle GreenLearning on YouTube. I recommend you check out his work. He felt that anyone could grow enough food for one person on 4,000 square feet of land (or ocean). He uses greenhouse techniques, vertical growing and fisheries amongst the vegetables.

What's the maximum population possible? How much food could be produced on Earth? A few simple calculations, excluding Greenland, Antarctica and mountainous terrain (estimated at about 24% of the total), we arrive at a rough maximum of about 359.36 billion people. Certainly, we might cut back on this figure a fair amount to allow for pathways, transportation, and other land use.

Would Earth ever get that many people? I doubt it. As stated earlier, as populations become more prosperous, the birth rates go down. Some countries have shrinking population levels. And these are the more prosperous countries, like Japan. In 2010, the census gave a figure of 128 million Japanese. By 2050, the population is expected to have dropped to 95 million.

Fearless Confidence in the Spirit of Man

We need to remain fearless. We should never react to alarmist rhetoric. Instead, we should take any warning, and use restraint before judging, pro or con. And we should investigate deeply before acting. But always, we should be ready to admit that we were wrong, if ever we discover that we were. New data can sometimes make our prior "truth" into a "lie."

To solve the problems of the world, we start out by facing our fears and separating the truly troublesome from the far larger array of inconsequential facts. When you see the bigger picture, you start to see people's motivations. When that happens, fear frequently disappears.

Chapter 2: The Current Ice Age

"Definition of a banker: A man who loans you an umbrella when the sun is shining, asks for it back at the first sprinkle of rain, and doesn't own the umbrella in the first place."—Swen Teresed, Deseret News, *November 9, 1949*

Yes, we're in an Ice Age and have been for 2.6 million years. It all started with the persistence of polar ice throughout the year. That's for both poles. Antarctica received a head start when ice started accumulating there over 30 million years ago. For most of Earth's history, the poles have been free of ice. In other words, the norm is "warmth," not "cold."

And don't be confused by the fact that we have tropics with palm trees. We still live in an Ice Age as defined by those two little white things at the poles.

During the last 500 million years, there have been only four periods of extreme cold on Earth. These periods were approximately,

- 450–430Mya—At the start of the Silurian period (20 million years).
- 320–260Mya—From mid-Carboniferous to mid-Permian periods (60 million years).

- 160–130Mya—From late-Jurassic to early-Cretaceous periods (30 million years). The depths of this "cool" period were far warmer than today, and far warmer than what the IPCC projects for a century from now. Perhaps calling this "cool period" an Ice Age is a bit of a misnomer.
- 2.6Mya to Present (2.6 million years of climate controlled by ice).

Out of the last 500 million years, only about 112.6 million years have been relatively cold. Thirty million of those years were far warmer than anything the IPCC (United Nation's Intergovernmental Panel on Climate Change) has imagined. Yet that thirty million year period was a massive temperature slump from the periods on either side of it.

Estimates range from 7 to 12 degrees Celsius warmer than today for nearly 390 million years. Two major hot spots were up to 20 °C warmer than today—the Permian-Triassic and Cretaceous hothouse climates.

An Ice Age consists of glacial and interglacial periods. Glacials are long periods of massive cold that currently last about 90,000 years. They are characterized by enlarged glaciers covering much of North America and Europe. Along with the glaciers, we have far more deserts, extremely scarce rain, and greatly reduced populations. Interglacials are shorter periods of relative warmth, each lasting about 11,000 years on average. But this is only slightly warmer, resulting in glaciers which still remain, but in a far smaller footprint.

Global Warming is Good

When people normally look at the cracks in a dry riverbed, they think of heat evaporating all that water that used to be there. They think of hot desert climate. This happens on a local scale, but increasing warmth globally means more rainfall and more green.

Instead of global warming giving us more desert, it could give us far less desert. Why? Because most of the Earth is covered in oceans. More warmth means more evaporation there, too. More evaporation, means more water vapor, and, all other things being equal, more clouds and more rainfall. Of course, more rain means more plants growing and thus, smaller deserts.

During the early Holocene Epoch—during what is called the Holocene Optimum—the Sahara was green. The far warmer climate, plus monsoon patterns allowed that extra moisture to cover the Sahara, turning it into a grassland. Vast herds of animals migrated across it. How do we know? Early humans left pictures of these in what is now barren desert.

We currently live far closer to dangerous frozen climate than we are to any dangerous heat.

If average global climate were to drop by 2 °C, then we would suffer another Little Ice Age, like that of the 1300–1800s where crops failed, people were miserable in the cold, and massive storms became more frequent and violent. The Great Storm of 1703 is a perfect example of unusually violent weather, with 120 mph winds striking Great Britain. One such strong storm in the Little Ice Age was responsible for sinking the Spanish Armada in 1588. Global cooling ruined Spanish plans for world dominance.

Because storms depend on thermal potential (temperature differences), if the poles warm up enough to melt all that ice, then their temperatures will be far closer to those of the equatorial regions. Without a strong temperature difference, storms could virtually disappear. Heat isn't the only ingredient required for storms. You must have relative warmth and cold near each other.

We will look more closely at this in the chapter on extreme weather, "The Missing Global Warming Catastrophes."

Global Average Temperature is Difficult to Measure

What many people on both sides of this debate never seem to talk about is the fact that measuring the average global temperature is not easy. Also, the accuracy of our measurements remains highly questionable. For instance, there are thousands of temperature monitoring stations in the United States and Western Europe, but the rest of the world is disproportionately under-represented. How can you get an accurate picture of average global temperature if you don't take the temperature in most of the locations on Earth? Oops!

The largest gaping hole in the temperature record are the oceans. This is 70% of the Earth's surface and it remains the least represented area. Double oops!

Surface thermometers are also highly problematic, because they belong to a volunteer group and standards are poorly met. For instance, several ground thermometer stations were found on or near asphalt parking lots. One was found near air-conditioning exhaust vents. Lots of artificial warming to skew the temperature record. Triple oops!

Satellite data is perhaps the best temperature data, because of its thoroughness in covering the entire planet. It has its problems, but the clever climate scientists who work on the data are happy to make corrections as their peers discover discrepancies and problems with methodology.

The warming alarmists depend on the ground-based data, which is the poorest quality set of data. Even so, several governments have already been caught lowering older data and increasing newer data to make the temperature increase look more dramatic. That such a thing is happening in public makes it all the more surreal. The corrupt scientists have been caught red-handed, but the globalist-owned mainstream media does not report on this scandal.

Not only are the warming alarmists making wonderful warming out to be the bad guy, but they are also fudging the data to make it look as though more warming is happening than reality is showing us. That's one lie chasing another lie.

Chapter 3: Wonderful and Essential Carbon Dioxide

"Some people feel the rain; others just get wet."—Roger Miller, Lubbock Avalanche-Journal, *December 31, 1972*

Ever since this "global warming" scare took hold, carbon dioxide has been made out to be some kind of bad guy. When they talk about the increases in CO_2, it's all about industry creating "carbon pollution" or "greenhouse pollution."

Industry does pollute, some far more than others. But that's not everything industry produces. Some of the products industry produces are likely sitting in your own home, unless you live in a cave or a mud hut. Industry also outputs lots of excess water vapor, but we don't scream "water is pollution" because of it. We don't demand that people reduce their water footprint. And water vapor is a far more potent greenhouse gas in Earth's atmosphere because there is so much of it.

Ironically, carbon dioxide is not, and never has been a pollutant. It's a natural, colorless and essential gas of life. It is not toxic. We breathe it every day. In fact, humans exhale carbon dioxide, like all animal forms of life.

Carbon Dioxide (CO_2) is Good

CO_2 levels have averaged far higher than today. We've been in a CO_2 slump for several million years. For the last 75 million years, carbon dioxide levels have been below 1,000ppm. Today, we're back up to about where we were 5 million years ago. From 270–350 Mya, CO_2 levels were below 1,000ppm (parts per million by volume), every other time in Earth's history, CO_2 levels were far higher. From about 180–130 Mya, CO_2 levels were above 2,000ppm, hovering around 2500ppm for ten million years. Before 350 Mya, the average was about 3,000ppm, going as high as 4500ppm.

Right now, Earth is coming out of carbon dioxide starvation. The increases in carbon dioxide have been greening the Earth. It's ironic that so-called "green" groups, including Greenpeace, seem to be against carbon dioxide, despite the benefits of having a greener planet. If CO_2 levels were to fall to 140ppm, nearly all life on Earth would die. Only anaerobic microbes would survive. Approximately 30 million years ago, when CO_2 levels had dropped to 800ppm (twice our current levels), plants were so stressed by the carbon dioxide starvation, they evolved C4 species.

We have far more room for carbon dioxide expansion before we encounter any kind of dangerous saturation. Certainly, not every organism is going to respond the same way to any environmental changes, but by-and-large, CO_2 increases of up to 2,000ppm would prove beneficial, overall.

Humans use extra CO_2 in greenhouses all the time to increase crop production. If you think there's a danger, you're likely thinking of carbon dioxide's evil cousin, carbon _mon_oxide. As we've already mentioned, NASA has set the space station CO_2 limit to be 5,000ppm. Naval submarines use 8,000ppm CO_2 concentration. Carbon dioxide is an extremely safe gas.

In the last 300 years, humans have helped to push CO_2 concentration away from dangerous death levels. Bravo, humans!

Carbon Dioxide Forced to Wear a Scary Mask

From the very beginning of the thermophobia epidemic—this fear of global warming—carbon dioxide has been called many names and shunned by gentile society. CO_2 has been called "carbon pollution" (as if it were soot), "greenhouse pollution" or simply "pollution."

Because some of it comes from industry, it was viewed as evil. And all things produced by industry are evil, right? If you're reading this, then you're using a product of industry, whether this book is in print or electronic. So, does that make you evil? With every breath you take, you exhale carbon dioxide. Pollution is escaping from your nose and mouth. Evil, evil you! And because oxygen contributes to the creation of carbon dioxide, it must be evil, too. Reduce your oxygen footprint—destroy all plant life!

Okay, now let's get serious about this. Don't you see how ridiculous all this slander has become?

Now, the globalists want to tax carbon. That's not soot, but carbon dioxide. Carbon tax means that you pay the government for everything you use that was manufactured using fossil fuels. Where does that money go? Who benefits? In the United States, it would go to the central bank, the very private, Federal Reserve System. Not actually the government! This means, the bankers get richer while everyone else is burdened by a new tax. If the purpose of this tax were to decrease our carbon footprints, do you think it would work? Or would people grudgingly pay more for the conveniences they already have? We would get more CO_2 in the atmosphere, economies would suffer and bankers would get richer. Do you see a problem with this picture?

A more insidious problem with carbon tax is that the globalists gain more control over our lives. Far more valuable than the money that they make off of this scam is the leverage or influence they have over governments. It's actually quite clever. If anyone ever wanted to take over the planet, this may be a perfect method to accomplish that end.

Perhaps the cleverest side of the carbon tax scam is the notion that people learn not to trust those who warn about climate problems. In the 70s we saw warnings about a "New Ice Age." Now, we see warnings about Global Warming. And with the global warming "pause," people are starting to get fed up with it all. What if a real climate problem lurked around the corner? What if the Holocene were to end in the next few decades? How many people would die because of this problem: Is the "Boy Who Cried Wolf" syndrome making everyone skeptical of any and all climate warnings? Could this be the main goal of the "climate change" scam? But that would mean that the goal of this scam would be to kill off hundreds of millions or even billions of people. We will investigate this nasty idea in greater depth, later in the book.

But carbon dioxide isn't the only one in the lineup of suspects. Methane has also been forced to wear a scary mask. We now have some governments taxing cattle for their cow farts. Methane is a far more potent greenhouse gas by volume than either water vapor or carbon dioxide. This dangerous stuff must be stopped. Poor Bessie needs to hold her farts or cost her owner dearly.

How would you like a cork stopper shoved up your bum? But don't worry, your farts aren't going to destroy the world.

Will oxygen be the next gas to fall prey to this madness. After all, it does aid in the production of carbon dioxide (oxide is an alias for oxygen).

Al Gore Revisited

We've already looked at the fact that Al Gore's doubly award-winning film contains an infamous graph showing carbon dioxide levels and temperature levels for the last 650,000 years. At this scale there is a strong correlation shown between CO_2 and temperature. As mentioned earlier, temperature leads CO_2 by several hundred years. Warmer weather heats up the oceans and forces the dissolved carbon dioxide out into the atmosphere.

One proponent of the climate change scare produced a series of informative videos filled with half-truths. He makes the valid point that while CO_2 could have followed temperature increases, it could still have contributed to more warming. And the big question here is, "So what?"

The real question needs to be, "How strong is the CO_2 forcing of temperature?" If carbon dioxide is very strong, then it will force temperature to rise, creating more water vapor from evaporation, which warms the Earth even more, which causes more evaporation and CO_2 outgassing from the oceans, and so on, and so on. This could lead to a runaway greenhouse effect which boils the oceans and burns up the Earth.

But it never happened!

We have two pieces of evidence which throw a monkey wrench into that fear of warmth. Prepare yourself for some big, thermophobia medicine.

Temperatures have increased for the last 250 years or so, coming out of the Little Ice Age. But temperatures have also decreased several times during that period. In the last chapter, we saw a 60-year cycle clearly apparent in the temperature data of the last 150 years—thirty years up, thirty years down or leveled off.

- 1880–1910—cooling
- 1910–1940—warming
- 1940–1970—cooling
- 1970–2000—warming
- 2000–2016—level and possibly slight cooling

During all this time, CO_2 continued to rise somewhat steadily. The average global temperature seemed impervious to the inexorable climb in CO_2 concentrations. In other words, something else was driving average global temperatures—not CO_2.

There was a time, in the distant past, when CO_2 concentrations were on the order of 210,000ppm. This was when there was little or no pure oxygen in the atmosphere. This was before photosynthetic plants had evolved for converting CO_2 into food and oxygen. We did not have runaway greenhouse heating at that time. It looks as though carbon dioxide is not the 800 pound bully people make it out to be.

During the Cretaceous Thermal Maximum, about 94 million years ago, global average temperatures were said to have been 20 °C warmer than today. CO_2 levels were as much as 4,000ppm (10x today's levels). If carbon dioxide were such a strong driver, could temperatures ever have cooled to where they are today? Why didn't Earth simply burn up? Perhaps it's because there are sufficient negative feedbacks built into nature to help cool off the planet when things try to get too warm.

The two key negative feedbacks come from water vapor—guilty for about 95% of Earth's greenhouse warming effects. When water evaporates from the oceans, it cools things off. Lick your hand and wave it energetically. Feel the cooling effect? That's evaporation. The other negative feedback happens when that water vapor reaches a high altitude—high enough to turn into cloud droplets. Clouds shade the planet, reflecting large quantities of solar light back into space. That increases the cooling effect.

Carbon Dioxide Greening the Planet

We've already looked at the notion that carbon dioxide is greening the Earth, but this isn't some hypothetical situation or wishful thinking. Scientists, pouring over years of satellite data, have determined a measurable increase in plant growth from modern increases in CO_2. Journalist, James Taylor, writing for *Forbes* stated, "The findings, published in *Geophysical Research Letters*, are gleaned from satellite measurements of global plant life, and contradict assertions by activists that global warming is causing deserts to expand, along with devastating droughts." Scientists call it a "fertilization effect."

Not only are plants gaining in bulk and producing more food, they are also gaining in the ability to grow in harsher environments with less water. From 1982 to 2010, arid regions of the globe enjoyed an 11% increase in foliage.

Princeton University professor, Freeman Dyson, a world-renowned physicist, recently stated, "I like carbon dioxide, it's very good for plants. We know sort of the non-climate effects of carbon dioxide are good—they're very strong. It's good for the vegetation, it's good for the natural vegetation as well as for the farms."

Writing for *The Daily Caller*, Michael Bastasch stated, "A 2014 study by U.S. researchers found a 'substantial increase in water-use efficiency in temperate and boreal forests of the Northern Hemisphere over the past two decades.'"

ScienceDaily.com added, in an article on a CSIRO Australia study, "If elevated CO_2 causes the water use of individual leaves to drop, plants in arid environments will respond by increasing their total numbers of leaves. These changes in leaf cover can be detected by satellite, particularly in deserts and savannas where the cover is less complete than in wet locations, according to Dr. Donohue" (CSIRO research scientist, Dr. Randall Donohue).

The bottom line: Carbon dioxide (CO_2) has been vindicated. Increases in carbon dioxide are not only good for plant growth and food production, but they are also helping to reduce the size of deserts. Any measurable effect carbon dioxide has on global warming is also good, because, as we've seen, global warming is good, too.

Chapter 4: 'Climate Change' and Other Squishy Terms

"The ultimate weather forecast—the weather will continue to change, on and off, for a long, long time."—George Carlin, "George Carlin Again," 1978

Confusion Over the Term "Climate Change"

No one ever talks about "climate change" getting better. If the planet cooled, that would be climate change. If the planet warmed, that would be climate change. But both are bad? So, our current climate is good? If so, why are there so many complaints about it? What would they prefer? If they prefer something other than our current climate, then climate would need—oh!—to change to something else! But they said "climate change" was bad.

The big problem started out being called "global warming," but when the warming stopped, "climate change" became the predominant term. What remains ironic is the fact that the bad guy of climate change is still CO_2. But carbon dioxide supposedly causes global warming. Now, it supposedly causes "climate change," whatever that is.

Science has its definition of "climate change," but the United Nations and Al Gore have an entirely different definition. For the scientist, climate change means merely global warming, global cooling, fast changes, slow changes, steep changes and shallow changes. But "climate change" can also include changes in atmospheric composition, turbulence and any other physical characteristic which can be measured. This goes for any and all global average climate conditions over the last 4.5 Billion years—ever since Earth gained an atmosphere.

To the globalists — United Nations, Al Gore, Rockefellers and their ilk—"climate change" refers only to a rather limited and recent phenomenon caused only by humans. Specifically, it refers to catastrophic, man-made global warming from the use of CO_2-producing fossil fuels. The difference between the two terms is huge. In a very real sense, the scientific term has been kidnapped and, like carbon dioxide, forced to wear a scary mask. "Climate change" has been slandered and those who started the slander have millions of willing accomplices who do not know what they're doing.

When someone proclaims that we need to "stop climate change," they're being a touch moronic. Why? Because stopping "climate change" is a bit like "chaining the wind," or "stopping Earth in its orbit about the sun," or even "stopping the galaxies from spinning." Climate has always changed and always will. Humans have nothing to do with that. Absolutely zero! Humans may contribute a tiny amount to existing climate change, but humans are not responsible for all climate change. But this "guilty humans" idea is what the media, United Nations and Al Gore seem to want people to think— that the entirety of "climate change" is a human problem.

Quite simply, this is not true. If you were to take humans out of the equation altogether, climate would continue to change, because climate change is not a human activity, but a natural activity.

As we will discuss in chapter 8, nature has cycles of warming and cooling, and our Modern Warm Period is merely one of many such warm periods scientists have documented.

Why would someone kidnap a scientific term? This is not an easy question to answer. We will attempt to look at some possible answers in chapter 12.

Name Calling Madness—Climate Denial

When one side of a debate is losing, it seems all too typical these days that they fall back to using bad language and name calling. Those who disagree with their hysteria are "deniers." But deny what? The parallel with "Holocaust deniers" seems painfully obvious and underhanded. This approach won't work with anyone who has good critical thinking skills. So, why is it working at all? Because too many people are lousy at critical thinking. Even your author is gradually getting better at it.

Let's look closer at this idea of "denial."

Sometimes it's called simply, "climate denial" or "climate change denial." But what is being denied? In a convention of climate realists and skeptics, a similar question was asked with enlightening results.

When asked, "Who does not believe that climate is changing?" no one raised their hand. Amongst the audience members, there was a 100% consensus that climate was indeed changing. Not a "climate denier" in the lot.

When asked, "Who does not believe that the Earth has warmed since the 1950s?" again, no one raised their hand. Everyone believed in the warming which has occurred.

The audience was asked, "Who does not believe that man has released a significant amount of carbon dioxide into the atmosphere?" Again, no one raised their hand. Again, 100% consensus. No "climate denial." And all of these people have been accused of being "climate deniers."

Then, the audience was asked, "Who does not believe that man has contributed to climate change?" And again, no one raised their hand. Everyone in the audience agreed that humans have contributed at least something to the existing climate change.

The term "climate denial" is thus a slander based on lies. Not only that, it's based on a corrupted definition of a scientific term. So, while most everyone agrees with the scientific term, "climate change," the kidnapped and corrupted term used by the United Nations is where the disagreement exists.

So, what is this disagreement? For one, we disagree that humans are the only cause of climate change. The United Nations IPCC has concentrated only on human-caused climate change. That seems to be their mission. With such a narrow focus, no wonder their publications are so biased. They're only looking at data that confirms their agenda. We disagree that humans are the major cause of climate change. Climate has been changing—sometimes quite drastically—without any help from humans. In fact, at the end of the Younger Dryas "Big Freeze," nearly 12,000 years ago, climate suddenly warmed significantly, bouncing back from a 1,300-year return to Ice Age glacial conditions. Sea level rise had slowed significantly during the Younger Dryas period. Within 50 years, sea levels were rising again at nearly 7 feet per century.

And that was at the beginning of our Holocene interglacial. All that warming made civilization possible.

Humans contribute something to the climate. There is no denying that. The big question is, "How much?" The science is definitely not settled on this. On this there is very little consensus.

Ironically, though, it would be nice if humans did have more of an effect on climate. If they could warm the globe with CO_2 output, then we might be saved from the next Ice Age glacial period when the Holocene finally ends. Trust me: Frozen climate is a bitch.

Settled Science

The notion being promoted broadly that "climate" science is settled is utter nonsense. Any and all science is never settled. There is always more to learn. Nature is extremely complex, especially non-linear systems like climate and the weather.

Why would anyone ever claim that the science is settled? Why would anyone ever lie about something this big? The most obvious reason is to tell people to "shut up."

Imagine this: You have some information to contribute to an important discussion, but people keep telling you that they already have it all figured out. In other words, "shut up and don't bother us with details." What's at work, here? Could this be the difference between arrogance and humility? Or does someone have a hidden agenda? Hidden agendas do exist, you know. Our planet is not entirely devoid of criminals.

Scientific Consensus

Science is never done by consensus. That scientists agree has no bearing on science. No one should ever have declared Newton's theories of motion to be "laws." That was a very "consensus" thing to do, but it was very "anti-science."

For over a thousand years, people believed that the Earth was at the center of the universe. That was the consensus. Consensus did not make it right. Consensus blocked free inquiry. Consensus is anti-science.

Like the notion of "settled science," science by "consensus" also has the subtext: "shut up." It is meant to stop discussion.

Not long ago, it was announced that 2015 was the warmest year on record. This was despite the satellite records showing that global average temperatures have remained relatively flat for nearly two decades. Certainly, there have been some ups and downs, but the overall trend for the period 1999–2015 was relatively level, if not slightly down (cooler).

When a similar declaration was made in January 2015, about the year 2014 being the warmest year on record, David Rose, writing for *Mail on Sunday*, stated, "The Nasa climate scientists who claimed 2014 set a new record for global warmth last night admitted they were only 38 per cent sure this was true. ...subject to a margin of error. Nasa admits this means it is far from certain that 2014 set a record at all" (WattsUpWithThat.com).

Cooking the Books for Consensus

The fact that NASA has a web page promoting scientific "consensus" remains one of the low points in that agency's long history in support of science and exploration. On that website, they list the rather dubious study by Cook, *et al*, claiming a 97% consensus amongst climate scientists on the topic of "climate change" — whatever that means.

Cook's paper has a number of things wrong with it, not the least of which is that he and his team tossed most of their data. Can we say, "Oops?" The authors of some of the papers reviewed by Cook's team have stated publicly that Cook wrongly assessed their papers. That's bad enough, but Cook and his team won't release all of their data. In science, replication of results is an important concept. If others cannot duplicate the results, then the original hypothesis stands on shaky ground. When the authors of a study won't release their data, other scientists can't check their work and the results become essentially worthless. They become unverifiable claims. For a researcher to hide their data is anti-science.

In a 2013 blog post, Anthony Watts quotes an open letter from Richard Tol to Peter Høj, Vice-chancellor of the University of Queensland, where John Cook is employed. Tol is a professor of the economics of climate change at the Vrije Universiteit Amsterdam. In his letter, Tol remarks that he attempted on numerous occasions to acquire Cook's climate data and had received only a small percentage. He remarked, "I found that the consensus rate in the data differs from that reported in the paper. Further research showed that, contrary to what is said in the paper, the main validity test in fact invalidates the data. And the sample of papers does not represent the literature. That is, the main finding of the paper is incorrect, invalid and unrepresentative."

For instance, Cook's paper did not reveal what measures, if any, were taken to ensure their reviewers were unbiased. This by itself is a major flaw. Tol offered to help in that regard, but Cook's team members stated that reviewer confidentiality was at stake. Tol countered that he was willing to sign a "standard confidentiality agreement," but Cook and his team continued to refuse. After months of refusal, Tol then went over Cook's head with the open letter.

Careful analysis of Cook's paper reveals that their claims involve the idea that humans cause some global warming. Yet, this somehow translates into "most global warming" which is "catastrophic" in nature. Most climate scientists would likely agree that humans cause some global warming, but not nearly as many would agree with "most global warming" or "catastrophic."

It's almost as if the meme is what is important, and the truth doesn't matter. When an American president Tweets, "Ninety-seven percent of scientists agree: #climate change is real, man-made and dangerous," it doesn't matter if the report upon which the Tweet is based is flawed. What's important is keeping up the illusion of saving the planet. And when the actions would actually harm life on this planet, the irony of the meme deepens.

Cook and his team were not the only ones to come up with the "97%" sound bite. Lawrence Solomon, writing in 2011 for the *Financial Post,* states, "The number stems from a 2008 master's thesis by student Maggie Kendall Zimmerman at the University of Illinois, under the guidance of Peter Doran, an associate professor of Earth and environmental sciences. The two researchers obtained their results by conducting a survey of 10,257 Earth scientists. The survey results must have deeply disappointed the researchers — in the end, they chose to highlight the views of a subgroup of just 77 scientists, 75 of whom thought humans contributed to climate change. The ratio 75/77 produces the 97% figure that pundits now tout."

When scientists ignore most of the data and pick a vastly smaller subset in order to draw their conclusions, they have betrayed science. Would you hire someone who had applied such shady practices in their master's thesis?

Big Oil Playing Both Sides

In the few years I've been following the climate debate, one claim continues to rear its ugly head on social media—that "Big Oil" is funding the deniers. For the public-at-large, this works, because it's big, evil industry selfishly protecting itself.

Ironically, they don't pick up on the fact that they're getting their information from corporations owned by the same corrupt individuals.

To expect a scorpion or a snake not to sting or bite is entirely naive. Corporations remain selfish by their very nature. But to expect that corporate officers are unsophisticated bumpkins is also naive. In any conflict, the most sophisticated approach is one of supporting both sides in order to control the outcome. Biggest Oil Rockefellers have recently divested themselves of their oil holdings (Goldenberg), because it looks hypocritical for them to be supporting the warming alarmist's position and still to be making profit off of fossil fuels. Good move, but waiting until 2014 seems to contradict their commitment to the Carbon Tax scam and to the "man-made, catastrophic global warming" meme.

The strategy of playing both sides is an old one. The Rothschilds used it in eighteenth and nineteenth century Europe, funding both sides of each war. The Rothschild family had banks in all the major countries of the time—England, Germany, Austria, Italy and France. The Rockefellers made use of the same strategy in the Vietnam War and possibly others. In fact, Nelson Rockefeller, when being vetted for the vice president position under Gerald Ford, was asked about one of his companies supplying the enemy. Rockefeller claimed ignorance and the matter was closed. Paradoxically, treason was not enough of a motive to pursue the line of questioning. This is reminiscent of the recent treatment of Hillary Clinton over her criminal activities. For most of us, ignorance of the law is not an excuse. Neither is a lack of wrongful intent. A crime is still a crime. People like Clinton and Rockefeller work by a different set of rules.

If the enemy is "big, bad corporations," and those same corporations   attack   the   Rockefellers   (owners   of   big corporations), then the famous family must be good. Right? And if someone unethical is smart enough to understand this effect in human nature, don't you think they could use it to their own advantage? Even psychopaths can pretend to be victims. So, don't discount this possibility.

Chapter 5: The Missing Global Warming Catastrophes

"...the wheel what squeaks the loudest, is the one what gets the grease." —Cal Stewart, 1903

One of the biggest reasons to fear Global Warming involves extreme weather events—tornadoes and hurricanes.

What some people don't seem to understand is that wind (one dangerous ingredient in storms) is not caused by heat. Wind blows only when there is a temperature difference.

For those who think wind requires heat, please consider the colder planets in our own Solar system. For instance, Jupiter is a very cold planet with average temperatures of –108 °C at the level of 1 atmosphere of pressure. Yet, Jupiter has massive storms, some of which are larger than the entire planet Earth! The reason such extreme cold can drive such massive and energetic storms is because of thermal potential—very cold air adjacent to extreme cold. The temperature difference is what drives the storms.

Air that has no temperature differences doesn't know where to go. For example, Venus is a very hot planet—hot enough to melt lead—yet it has had almost no wind for millions of years. Why? Because the poles are nearly the same temperature as the equator. Midnight is nearly the same temperature as noon. Meteor craters formed millions of years ago remain in pristine condition, because there is practically no wind erosion. The surface of Venus remains a stifling, stagnant and scorching heat. Storms there are virtually non-existent on the entire planet's surface.

Now, that we have a sense for how storms get their energy, let's look at specific data on storm frequency.

Hurricanes and Typhoons

Scientists have tracked not only the number of tropical cyclones ("hurricanes" in the Atlantic and "typhoons" in the Pacific), they have also measured the total accumulated energy from the storms. Both are showing a downward trend. Dr. Ryan N. Maue published two graphs September 30, 2014 which show these effects. "Global Tropical Cyclone Accumulated Cyclone Energy (ACE)" shows a 20-year downward trend in both global and northern hemisphere measurements. The global measurement peaked in late 1993 at about 2,100 ACE (104 knots2), to about 1,300 ACE throughout 2014.

In a similar graph of hurricane counts, Dr. Maue shows a 22-year downward trend in "major hurricanes (those with speeds greater than or equal to 96 knots), and a 43-year downward trend in total hurricane counts (global).

We understand why storm wind energy is down and we have the evidence (facts) to back it up.

Tornadoes

NOAA (National Oceanic and Atmospheric Administration) graphs of tornadoes show a similar problem with the "climate change" hysteria. First of all, the total tornado counts—EF1 and stronger, from 1954 to 2014, shows a lot of up and down, but a rather flat trend. It should be pointed out that the smaller, weaker tornadoes are now far easier to document and count, because population density has increased and instrumentation has improved. So, the actual counts in the past could have missed a great many of the weaker tornadoes, because no one was around to measure them. The count in 1954 was about 440. In 1963, the count had dipped to about 340. From that point, there was a strong upward trend to 1973, when the count stood at about 880. Then, the counts plummeted to a low of about 350 in 1978. The next few decades saw counts rise and fall, never getting above 700, and dipping as low as 310 in 2002. The approximate counts for the subsequent years were as follows:

- 2004 — 600
- 2005 — 450
- 2006 — 420
- 2007 — 430
- 2008 — 710
- 2009 — 460
- 2010 — 510
- 2011 — 895
- 2012 — 370
- 2013 — 405
- 2014 — 410

As you can see, the counts were all over the place. The count in 2010 was only slightly greater than the peak in 1973.

Counts of stronger tornadoes are more reliable simply because strong tornadoes make themselves known with greater ferocity. The NOAA chart of F3–F5 tornadoes shows a strong downward trend for the last 40 years. Counts for 2012–2014 were all below 30. Counts from 1954–1977 never went below 30. The high count for the new millennium — 2011 at 83 — was exceeded five times in the period 1957–1974.

So, when the news media and government agencies talk of more and stronger storms caused by global warming, they not only do not understand the basic science behind wind, but have not done their homework by looking at the existing evidence.

Droughts

In Al Gore's *Inconvenient Lie,* he talks about droughts in Darfur and in Chad. He mentions that Lake Chad has dried up. He said that the lake was once a far larger body of water. And he's absolutely right about that. What he forgot to mention is that Lake Chad was nearly four times larger than it has been in modern times and more than a dozen meters deeper, making it a robust inland sea during the far warmer Holocene Optimum. During that same period, the Sahara was green. Signs of the ancient civilizations which had lived in the Sahara still exist—carvings and paintings, made during the three thousand year period of prosperity.

Quite rightly, Gore mentions that warmth creates more evaporation and sucks moisture out of the soil, but the balance is in favor of more rain, once the warming is well established. That's why the Sahara was green for three millennia.

Not every location is going to get this extra rain. There will still be deserts, some of them far drier than they are today. But extra water vapor means more rain all around.

Flooding

There has always been flooding, so reports of catastrophic flooding are being overblown to create more hysteria. If you dig through the modern reports of extraordinary flooding, a look into the past reveals that the current extremes were only repeats.

Manfred Mudelsee, *et al*, write that central Europe shows no upward trends in the occurrence of extreme floods. With records stretching back for more than 500 years, the worst is in the past.

The flooding on Meramec and Mississippi rivers in late December 2015 were the result of overbuilding and poor planning. This is according to Robert Criss, PhD, professor of earth and planetary sciences in Arts & Sciences at Washington University in St. Louis. The previous record flood on the Meramec in 1982 should have shown similarities to the 2015 flood, because both were winter floods during an El Niño event. But there were big differences. Upon investigation, Criss discovered a major levee had been built on the Meramec—three miles long. Also, a landfill had been expanded, and there had been major development along three small tributaries. Humans, building without regard to impact on water channeling, have created a monster, and then blamed it on the climate (Watts, 2016:0206).

Also in 2015, a flood in South Carolina was declared to have been a "1,000-year flood" by climate alarmists. The USGS, however, reported that, "The provisional peak flood flow that USGS measured for the Congaree River in Columbia was 185,000 cubic feet per second (cfs) on Sunday, October 4, 2015. The maximum recorded in history was 364,000 cfs in 1908, which is almost double what was experienced in this current flood" (Watts, 2015:1010).

A paper written by Dr. Madhav Khandekar, points out that floods like the September 2014 event in Kashmir are not unusual and are not tied to human created CO_2. Khandekar is a former meteorologist with the India Meteorological Department in Pune (India) and Environment Canada (Watts, 2014:1112).

A major flooding event, with 2.96 inches of rain in Phoenix, Arizona, September 8, 2014, was said to have been a record-breaker, beating out the 1933 record of 2.91 inches. Yet, Dr. Roger Pielke, Jr. observed that there is no climatic trend in floods. He shared via Twitter a NOAA chart of the Extreme Precipitation Index from 1900–2010. The highest index was in 1916. All levels from 1990–2010 were below the levels for 1909, 1914, 1919 and 1921 (Watts, 2014:0908).

Time after time, records show that the climate alarmists are wrong about an increase in floods.

Rising Oceans

The only major problem with global warming is that of rising oceans. That's inevitable, even if we had no more ice to melt. Why? Because warmth increases the volume of water. Heat expands most substances. Ice is one major exception. The oceans will expand simply by warming up. Melting of the current polar glaciers will result in roughly a 200-foot rise in sea levels, because much of that ice is currently on land.

But here's the tradeoff:

1) Either people move to higher ground and enjoy the warmer climate, fewer deserts, fewer and weaker storms, greater life-giving rain and more food, or

2) People suffer the extreme cold, massive loss of land from Ice Age glaciation, failed crops, massive starvation, rain scarcity, and massive increases in deserts and dust.

Some choice!

With global warming, some people are inconvenienced and zero die, unless people foolishly remain attached to real estate. With global cooling, in the midst of our ongoing Ice Age, billions could die, and humanity could suffer the loss of millions of square kilometers of land from glaciation and desertification. Either way, we lose land and people are inconvenienced. But with cooling, people are almost guaranteed to die, unless humanity prepares for the coming change.

Given a choice, the smart human would chose to support those measures which would help ensure greater survival. In part 3, "The Cure," we look at several suggestions for the only two viable directions for humanity—preparation for the cold (if necessary), and ending the Ice Age (if possible).

While it remains sad whenever people suffer because of storm surge or flooding, their choice to live next to the coast is part of the problem. With global warming, we can eliminate most, if not all storms. We can eliminate the source of extreme temperature differences—all that polar ice. As we learn from our mistakes, civilization will gain in maturity when it figures out how to work with nature. Any buildings along the coast might be temporary or movable, at least until the polar ice is gone. Even then, sea levels may rise and fall as global average temperature changes between various levels of warmth. Warmer water takes up more room.

Extreme Weather Lies

As we've seen, the warming alarmists—the source of thermophobia, our fear of warmth—have lied about extreme weather events. They have taken anecdotal evidence and blazoned it across the news media as if it meant something new and different.

When James Hanson first broached the topic of Global Warming to the United States Congress, he ensured he had their attention by having the air conditioning turned off on one of the warmest days of the year, right before his presentation (Goddard, 2012:0712).

Clever. But was it very ethical when the entire notion of "global warming" being bad is itself a lie?

Chapter 6: The Bad Boys—IPCC, Climate Gate and Mr. Hockey Stick

"...concerning New-England weather—it is a matter about which a great deal is said, but very little done."— Charles Dudley Warner, Proceedings of the Chamber of Commerce of the State of New York, *November 18, 1884*

Some groups talk a lot about climate, but don't do very much of value. In fact, the widely used term, "precautionary principle," is sometimes used to argue for any action being better than no action. But is this notion true? Can you think of an example where it remains false? How about a crowd standing near the Grand Canyon and everyone in the group decides to get a closer look, pushing those who are closest right over the edge! And because some are leaping to their deaths, others unknowingly follow them over the edge until it's too late to change their minds.

What would you think of someone who said that we all need to throw gasoline on a fire? What about someone who pushes the notion that we should cool down the planet in an ongoing Ice Age? Both of these actions seem no better than that of trying to convince a hungry man to fear food.

It should be already obvious that the precautionary principle is only as good as the direction in which it is aimed. But in today's environment of quick sound bites and knee-jerk reactions, the obvious needs to be repeated to help wake up the hypnotized and the mentally sluggish.

As incredible as it may seem, some scientists are in the game more for the money and fame, than for the advancement of science. These are the bad boys of science. The fact that their number is greater than zero is a tragedy. And yet, their numbers seem to be rising. Too many are tempted by the lure of funding. Even the more ethical scientists are finding that by merely adding the words "global warming" to their paper, they more easily get it published, even when their topic only tangentially touches on climate. Using the perverted term "climate change," a researcher can attract funding that might not otherwise be available to them. So, even the good scientists are spoiling the pot by spitting wads of goop into the mix. They are making science as a whole more dull-witted by using sloppy terminology and misplaced jargon. They are contributing to the misuse of terms and the distortion of our language.

Correspondence with a NASA Scientist

In July 2015, I noticed that NASA had a "consensus" page on the topic of climate. I wrote a letter of complaint stating, "Your use of 'scientific consensus' is incredibly unscientific, because science is never done by consensus." I also complained about NASA associating with the UN's notion of "climate change." I mentioned the Medieval Warm Period and the Holocene Optimum as examples of beneficial warming, including the greening of the Sahara.

The response I got back from one NASA scientist was cordial, but she completely ignored the part about "scientific consensus"—my main complaint. She explained what "climate change" meant to her, and seemed oblivious to the definition used in the UN's IPCC and the mainstream media. Her definition was pretty close to mine and quite scientific. She also said that the Medieval Warm Period and Holocene Optimum were not global events. She made it clear that 2005, 2010 and 2014 temperatures were the warmest on record.

I responded and reiterated my complaint about "scientific consensus." Still no reply on that point. I also supplied her with 21 sources (peer reviewed articles) which found both the Medieval Warm Period and Holocene Optimum to be global in scope, but no response to that, either. I pointed out the wording on NASA's climate consensus page, that it related the UN's definition of "climate change," not her scientific definition. I complained again that NASA was not using the proper definition of "climate change." No response to that. I pointed out that the ground-based data was highly suspect and pointed out the studies which had found that standards had not been kept for ground-based reporting stations. I reiterated the fact that we remain in an Ice Age and that global cooling proposed by the UN and NASA are thus irresponsible and dangerous. No response to that.

Ironically, the claim about "warmest year on record" is highly dubious. In January 2015, David Rose wrote in *Mail on Sunday*, "The Nasa climate scientists who claimed 2014 set a new record for global warmth last night admitted they were only 38 per cent sure this was true. ...subject to a margin of error. Nasa admits this means it is far from certain that 2014 set a record at all."

Gavin Schmidt, of NASA GISS, was questioned on whether or not he regretted not including the "margin of error" statement in their press release. He did not respond.

Who are the culprits behind this intellectual madness? And why are they doing it? We know only part of the answers to these questions. We have some speculation about their end-game, but it remains just that—speculation. Yet, the speculation is based on known facts. Let us look at some of those facts.

IPCC Fraud

Rajendra Pachauri, the former head of the IPCC, wrote: "For me the protection of Planet Earth, the survival of all species and sustainability of our ecosystems is more than a mission. It is my religion and my dharma." He believed this mantra so fervently that he was willing to lie to forward his agenda. And he wasn't the only one. When Dr. John Christy was an IPCC lead author in 2001, his fellow scientists were thrilled at the opportunity to lie and to distort the data to make it seem even worse than it was, just to sell the "climate change" scare.

Ironically, Pachauri had a PhD in the economics of railroad engineering and not a climate scientist. Christopher Booker, writing for the Telegraph, said, "Laughably described as 'the world's leading climate scientist', this absurd figure,... should never have been given the job in the first place. As a vegetarian, he jetted round the world exhorting everyone else to save the planet by giving up air travel and meat." Though his lack of climate training is not necessarily a fatal one, Pachauri proved to be a consummate liar.

Under Pachauri, the IPCC claimed that the Himalayan glaciers would have all but melted by 2035. The source was "an obscure Indian scientist quoted by the WWF." Booker went on to say, "...we were even more amazed to find that

Pachauri had hired the man responsible to be Teri's [The Energy and Resources Institute] chief glacier expert."

Pachauri ultimately stepped down from his lead position at the IPCC because of "allegations of sexual harassment by a young female employee of his Delhi research body, The Energy and Resources Institute (TERI), from which he has also now stepped down."

Climate-Gate and Sensitive Scientists

One of the places which supplies information to the United Nations' Intergovernmental Panel on Climate Change (IPCC) is the Climate Research Unit at the University of East Anglia. The university is located in Norwich, Norfolk, United Kingdom. Dr. Phil Jones has been the director of the CRU since 2004, and a joint director with Jean Palutikof 1998–2004.

In late 2009, computer hackers found their way onto the CRU's server and stole a great deal of data. Among the information taken were hundreds of emails which were subsequently posted online. Though the official story was that there was no evidence of scientific fraud or misconduct, others disagree.

As in America, Britain's Freedom of Information Act requires that publicly funded organizations like the CRU remain open and transparent. In response to an email from the former CRU director, Tom Wigley, January 21, 2005, Phil Jones wrote, "I wouldn't worry about the code. If FOIA does ever get used by anyone, there is also IPR to consider as well. Data is covered by all the agreements we sign with people, so I will be hiding behind them. I'll be passing any requests onto the person at UEA who has been given a post to deal with them."

Unlike most other scientists, Phil Jones makes a point of "hiding" behind the rules so their data and procedures will never make the light of day. So much for peer review and the high prized "reproducibility" in science. Without access to data and procedures, no one can check their results. Perhaps that was their intention all along.

Michael Mann, the scientist famous for bending the climatic data to form a "hockey stick" shaped graph by "hiding the decline" also refused to release his email data. Mann invoked the notion of "intellectual property" implying that, though his data was being used to set policy worldwide, no one had a right to know what it was.

The attorney who had requested Mann's emails stated his reasons, "These emails represent a period of time when the science upon which major national and international policies have been based was being done. In light of the extremely important public policy issues that these emails informed, the public has a right to know what these government employees were doing and how they were doing it" (Ball, 2015).

Some scientists had reported that global warming had taken a holiday after 1998, called by many as the "warming pause." In June 2015, NOAA employees (Tom Karl, *et al)* submitted a paper to *Science* entitled, "Possible artifacts of data biases in the recent global surface warming hiatus." Researcher Ross McKitrick found problems with their paper. McKitrick, with Steve McIntyre, had helped expose Michael Mann's "hockey stick" fraud. Others attempted to gain more information for clarification by Karl and his team refused. A congressional press release revealed problems in the govern-ment employees' openness. "Science, Space, and Technology Committee Chairman Lamar Smith (R-Texas) today sent a letter to National Oceanic and Atmospheric Administration (NOAA) Administrator Kathryn Sullivan responding to the agency's unjustified refusal to provide the Committee with documents related to the agency's decision to alter historical climate data. After three letters requesting these documents,

Chairman Smith issued a subpoena on October 13th to obtain communications related to NOAA's decision."

But the government agency's scientists did not respond. Not long afterward, the agency offered an explanation: "Although NOAA failed to provide the Committee with any justification for withholding documents, a NOAA spokeswoman was quoted in the media saying that the agency's 'internal communications are confidential and not related to what Smith is trying to find out.' As such, NOAA reportedly does not intend to provide the Committee with communications."

The highest legal body of the land demanded documents from government employees and they refused. The agency also cited "confidentiality concerns and the integrity of the scientific process."

Since when does an employee refuse to show their work to their boss? Are publicly funded agencies allowed confidentiality to hid what may be crimes? Is scientific integrity something that evaporates under public scrutiny?

Congressman Smith, who had demanded the information from NOAA later revealed, "Whistleblowers have told the committee, according to Smith's letter, that Thomas Karl—the director of NOAA's National Centers for Environmental Information, which led the study—'rushed' to publish the climate study 'before all appropriate reviews of the underlying science and new methodologies' used in the climate data sets were conducted."

When scientists spend so much time hiding their work, you have to worry about the conclusions drawn from it all. Honest scientists have nothing to hide. They encourage others to dig through their dirty laundry of data and to pick it apart for possible mistakes. That way, everyone learns, and science grows. In this era of secrets, everyone loses but the criminals who hide behind procedures and rules.

Here is an example of one of Phil Jones's emails. In this one, he appears to be attempting to silence a Dr. Sonja Boehmer-Christiansen and to keep her from using her past affiliation with a former employer. No verification has been done to ensure this text is authentic, but Phil Jones has never denied the authenticity of the posted emails, either.

```
>---Original Message---
>From: Phil Jones [mailto:p.jones@xxxxxxxxx.xxx]
>Sent: 27 October 2009 17:05
>To: Graham F Haughton
>Subject: Dr Sonja BOEHMER-CHRISTIANSEN
>
>
> Dear Professor Haughton,
> The email below was brought to my attention
>by the help desk of UKCP09 - the new set of UK
>climate scenarios developed for DEFRA. It was
>sent by the person named in the header of this
>email. I regard this email as very malicious. Dr
>Boehmer-Christiansen states that it is beyond
her
>expertise to assess the claims made. If this is
>the case then she shouldn't be sending malicious
>emails like this.
...[snipped]...
> I'm sure you will be of the same opinion as
>me that science should be undertaken through the
>peer-review literature as it has been for over
>300 years. The peer-review system is the
>safeguard science has developed to stop bad
science being published.
...[snipped]...
> I realize Dr Boehmer-Christensen no longer
>works for you, but she is still using your
affiliation.
>
> Best Regards
> Phil Jones
```

Graham Haughton responded to Jones commenting about her use of past affiliation, "*...at the moment in fairness she is entitled to use it in the way she does.... But as with all academics,*

I'd want to protect another academic's freedom to be contrary and critical, even if I personally believe she is probably wrong."

And Jones sent one last email to thank Haughton for his "speedy reply." He wrote, in part, *"You are probably aware of this, but the journal Sonja edits is at the very bottom of almost all climate scientists lists of journals to read. It is the journal of choice of climate change skeptics and even here they don't seem to be bothering with journals at all recently. I don't think there is anything more you can do. I have vented my frustration and have had a considered reply from you."*

When Jones's request failed to get the desired result, he inserted a barb of negativity to demean Boehmer-Christiansen's work and her then current employer. What a guy, Phil. You really know how to make friends and influence people.

Ironically, Phil Jones had remarked about the importance of peer review, but proved time and again that he was only paying lip service to the idea. He wanted to hide his data and procedures from the prying eyes of skeptics, but was quite willing to share with his buddies, because each of them listed each other as potential peer reviewers whenever they submitted a new article for publication. When only your buddies are your peer reviewers, how do you ever get a truly objective assessment of your work?

In another email, Michael Mann writes Phil Jones with thoughts on how to ruin a science journal that has published articles with opposing ideas. Their cozy club is creating a carbuncle on the back side of science.

```
From: "Michael E. Mann" <mann@xxxxxxxxx.xxx>
To:            Phil            Jones
<p.jones@xxxxxxxxx.xxx>,rbradley@xxxxxxxxx.xxx,
mhughes@xxxxxxxxx.xxx,srutherford@xxxxxxxxx.xxx,t
crowley@xxxxxxxxx.xxx
Subject: Re: Fwd: Soon & Baliunas
Date: Tue, 11 Mar 2003 08:14:49 -0500
```

Cc:
k.briffa@xxxxxxxxx.xxx,jto@u.arizona.edu,drdendro
@xxxxxxxxx.xxx,
keith.alverson@xxxxxxxxx.xxx,mmaccrac@xxxxxxxxx.x
xx,jto@u.arizona.edu, mann@xxxxxxxxx.xxx

Thanks Phil,
(Tom: Congrats again!)
The Soon & Baliunas paper couldn't have cleared a
'legitimate' peer review process
anywhere. That leaves only one possibility--that
the peer-review process at Climate
Research has been hijacked by a few skeptics on
the editorial board. And it isn't just De
Frietas, unfortunately I think this group also
includes a member of my own department...
The skeptics appear to have staged a 'coup' at
"Climate Research" (it was a mediocre
journal to begin with, but now its a mediocre
journal with a definite 'purpose').
Folks might want to check out the editors and
review editors:
[1]http://www.int-
res.com/journals/cr/crEditors.html
In fact, Mike McCracken first pointed out this
article to me, and he and I have discussed
this a bit. I've cc'd Mike in on this as well,
and I've included Peck too. I told Mike that
I believed our only choice was to ignore this
paper. They've already achieved what they
wanted--the claim of a peer-reviewed paper. There
is nothing we can do about that now, but
the last thing we want to do is bring attention
to this paper, which will be ignored by the
community on the whole...
It is pretty clear that thee skeptics here have
staged a bit of a coup, even in the
presence of a number of reasonable folks on the
editorial board (Whetton, Goodess, ...). My
guess is that Von Storch is actually with them
(frankly, he's an odd individual, and I'm
not sure he isn't himself somewhat of a skeptic
himself), and without Von Storch on their
side, they would have a very forceful personality
promoting their new vision.
There have been several papers by Pat Michaels,
as well as the Soon & Baliunas paper, that
couldn't get published in a reputable journal.

This was the danger of always criticising the
skeptics for not publishing in the
"peer-reviewed literature". Obviously, they found
a solution to that--take over a journal!
So what do we do about this? I think we have to
stop considering "Climate Research" as a
legitimate peer-reviewed journal. Perhaps we
should encourage our colleagues in the climate
research community to no longer submit to, or
cite papers in, this journal. We would also
need to consider what we tell or request of our
more reasonable colleagues who currently
sit on the editorial board...
What do others think?
mike

An article at Anthony Watts website gives 33 examples of emails that display questionable ethics, methods or morals on the part of the warming alarmist gang. The links to the email text no longer take us to the data, as it seems the website has since closed. But using http://archive.org, you can paste the URL into their search window and by clicking on the earliest archive saved, you can read the original text (Watts, 2009).

In still another email, Phil Jones showed his true colors concerning the death of one of his opposition scientists.

```
Subject: John L. Daly dead
Date: Thu, 29 Jan 2004 12:04:28 +0200
X-Mailer: Microsoft Outlook, Build 10.0.4510
Importance: Normal
```

Mike,
In an odd way this is cheering news ! One other
thing about the CC paper - just found
another email - is that McKittrick says it is
standard practice in Econometrics journals
to give all the data and codes !! According to
legal advice IPR overrides this.

Cheers
Phil

Cheering news? Certainly, happiness over the death of someone with whom you disagree is not a crime, but there's something seriously wrong with his humanity. The bit about "legal advice" and "IPR" refers to hiding information from others who might want to use it against them. The very fact that he feels the need to hide data shows he's not a true scientist in the spirit of open research and reproducibility.

And here's the infamous "hide the decline" email that has many climate scientists shaking their heads. Others claim that there's nothing wrong with what Jones, *et al*, have done, but you have to wonder about their biases. True skeptics would like to know what all Jones and his gang did, but when the CRU and their buddies don't feel like sharing, it's easy to suspect them of less than honorable actions.

```
From: Phil Jones
To: ray bradley ,mann@xxxxx.xxx, mhughes@xxxx.xxx
Subject: Diagram for WMO Statement
Date: Tue, 16 Nov 1999 13:31:15 +0000
Cc: k.briffa@xxx.xx.xx,t.osborn@xxxx.xxx
```

Dear Ray, Mike and Malcolm,
Once Tim's got a diagram here we'll send that either later today or
first thing tomorrow.

I've just completed Mike's Nature trick of adding in the real temps
to each series for the last 20 years (ie from 1981 onwards) amd from
*1961 for Keith's to **hide the decline**. Mike's series got the annual*
land and marine values while the other two got April-Sept for NH land
N of 20N. The latter two are real for 1999, while the estimate for 1999
for NH combined is +0.44C wrt 61-90. The Global estimate for 1999 with
data through Oct is +0.35C cf. 0.57 for 1998.

Thanks for the comments, Ray.

Cheers
Phil

The *Wall Street Journal* contained some interesting analysis of Jones and his buddies, based on the emails they had supposedly sent. Up front, they quote one of the emails: "The two MMs have been after the CRU station data for years. If they ever hear there is a Freedom of Information Act now in the U.K., I think I'll delete the file rather than send to anyone. . . . We also have a data protection act, which I will hide behind." And this from the same Phil Jones who said peer review was important? The journal also wrote, "...the university said it could not confirm that all the emails were authentic, though it acknowledged its servers were hacked"

Perhaps the most potent and poignant remark by the Wall Street Journal, in their article, speaks to the irony of the behavior of these scientists. Many of the scientists who the journal contacted for comments would not respond to their requests. "Yet all of these nonresponses manage to underscore what may be the most revealing truth: That these scientists feel the public doesn't have a right to know the basis for their climate-change predictions, even as their governments prepare staggeringly expensive legislation in response to them" (Wall Street Journal, 2009).

Think about that for a moment. Governments want to stick you and I with a multi-trillion dollar bill and loss of national sovereignty based on what Phil Jones and his buddies are "discovering," and Jones won't share. I'm not sure I'd want to pay all that "carbon" tax, even if Jones, *et al*, were entirely honest, cordial and transparent. But with their nasty attitudes and secretive nature, the answer is "Damn no!"

The sheer volume of emails downloaded, the details, pet names used, as well as the personal attitudes and behavior, all seem consistent with the Phil Jones and Michael Mann others have come to know.

James Randerson, writing for *The Guardian*, reported that the illegal actions taken by Jones and his crew were discovered too late to be punished. "Too late to take action, says deputy commissioner." Deputy Information Commissioner, Graham Smith commented on the poor handling by Jones and the CRU of Freedom of Information (FOI) requests. Randerson wrote, "Smith's statement refers to an FOI request from a retired engineer and climate sceptic in Northampton called David Holland.... In his statement, Smith said that Holland's request was not dealt with correctly by the university. 'The emails which are now public reveal that Mr Holland's requests under the Freedom of Information Act were not dealt with as they should have been under the legislation. Section 77 of the Freedom of Information Act makes it an offence for public authorities to act so as to prevent intentionally the disclosure of requested information.' But he added that it was now too late to take action because the legislation requires that sanctions are imposed within six months of the offence. 'The ICO is gathering evidence from this and other time-barred cases to support the case for a change in the law. It is important to note that the ICO enforces the law as it stands – we do not make it.'"

Writing for the Daily Mail, Rob Waugh quoted Phil Jones, "Any work we have done in the past is done on the back of the research grants we get – and has to be well hidden. I've discussed this with the main funder (U.S. Dept of Energy) in the past and they are happy about not releasing the original station data."

Interesting that a government agency would want scientific research, paid for by taxpayers, to remain hidden from the public. Again, Jones betrays his mistrust of real peer review. This time it wasn't in a hacked email he could claim he never wrote. This was a public statement to the press.

If the hacked emails can be trusted, then the computer programming code found might prove to be more of a verification of wrongdoing than all the emails put together.

Anthony Watts quotes a commenter named Neal at the climate audit website: "People are talking about the emails being smoking guns but I find the remarks in the code and the code more of a smoking gun. The code is so hacked around to give predetermined results that it shows the bias of the coder. In other words make the code ignore inconvenient data to show what I want it to show. The code after a quick scan is quite a mess. Anyone with any pride would be to ashamed of to let it out public viewing. As examples [of] bias take a look at the following remarks from the MANN code files:

```
function
mkp2correlation,indts,depts,remts,t,filter=filter,r
efperiod=refperiod,$
datathresh=datathresh
;
; THIS WORKS WITH REMTS BEING A 2D ARRAY
(nseries,ntime) OF MULTIPLE TIMESERIES
; WHOSE INFLUENCE IS TO BE REMOVED. UNFORTUNATELY
THE IDL5.4 p_correlate
; FAILS WITH >1 SERIES TO HOLD CONSTANT, SO I
HAVE TO REMOVE THEIR INFLUENCE
; FROM BOTH INDTS AND DEPTS USING MULTIPLE LINEAR
REGRESSION AND THEN USE THE
; USUAL correlate FUNCTION ON THE RESIDUALS.
;
pro maps12,yrstart,doinfill=doinfill
;
; Plots 24 yearly maps of calibrated (PCR-
infilled or not) MXD reconstructions
; of growing season temperatures. Uses
"corrected" MXD - but shouldn't usually
; plot past 1960 because these will be
artificially adjusted to look closer to
; the real temperatures.
;
```

The last sentence of the programmer's remarks is most telling. Even they put "corrected" in quotation marks to indicate the euphemistic intent; "fudged" or "faked" might be more truthful. Particularly telling are the words "artificially adjusted" indicating fraudulent intent to add non-natural data to achieve a desired result, rather than merely reporting on what nature provides.

Phil Jones told reporters that his emails were taken out of context. Perhaps they were. Or perhaps he's merely attempting to hide crimes any criminal would not want revealed. We don't entirely know. But the programmer's comments are far more unambiguous. As a programmer with more than 2 decades of experience, I know that remarks I make in my own code need to be clear so that any programmer can later understand the intent of the code and thus only make changes compatible with the original design and intent.

Anthony Watts sums it up very nicely when he wrote, "Either the data tells the story of nature or it does not. Data that has been 'artificially adjusted to look closer to the real temperatures' is false data, yielding a false result" (Watts, 2009:1122).

Putting Climate Gate into Perspective

Dr. Tim Ball on discussing the "climate gate" fiasco, said in an interview, "...professor Wegman, who was asked to arbitrate in the debate about the 'hockey stick,' he identified forty-two people and said, 'look, these people are all publishing together, and they're also peer-reviewing each other's literature.' So, there's a classic example of the kind of thing that had bothered me. About twenty years ago, I started to [ask], 'Well, why are they pushing the peer review issue so big? Why are they saying, 'Well, you haven't published peer review, and you haven't done this peer review.' And now, of course, we realize it's because they have control of their own process. And that's clearly exposed in these emails."

Ball's comments in the interview point out a major flaw in the peer review process, whereby submissions include recommendations of potential peer reviewers. When a group of scientists can depend on members of their own group to review favorably their own works, then the system is rigged to promote individual publication, rather than the advancement of science. That constitutes cronyism if not outright fraud (Corbett Report, 2009:1121).

Phil Jones and Michael Mann are not the only ones to use "hiding" data as a strategy for their kind of "science."

It seems one Jonathan Overpeck sent an email to the wrong person. Apparently, he mistook Dr. David Deming as a fellow warming alarmist. In a public statement presented to the United States senate on December 6, 2006, Deming said, "In 1995, I published a short paper in the academic journal *Science*. In that study, I reviewed how borehole temperature data recorded a warming of about one degree Celsius in North America over the last 100 to 150 years. The week the article appeared, I was contacted by a reporter for National Public Radio. He offered to interview me, but only if I would state that the warming was due to human activity. When I refused to do so, he hung up on me.

"I had another interesting experience around the time my paper in *Science* was published. I received an astonishing email from a major researcher in the area of climate change. He said, 'We have to get rid of the Medieval Warm Period.'" This last incident referred to the Overpeck email. Though Overpeck did not use those words, the meaning was the same. Deming merely paraphrased an overly long statement by Overpeck, though he did not mention Overpeck's name to the senate. Overpeck's original words were, "...I get the sense that

I'm not the only one who would like to deal a mortal blow to the misuse of supposed warm period terms and myths in the literature" (Watts, 2013:1208).

What seems ironic is the clear bias by the National Public Radio reporter who had contacted Deming. He only wanted to interview Deming if he would agree to blame humans for the warming. If you thought reporting was unbiased, this should wake you up.

The infamous "hockey stick" graph by Mann, *et al,* (1998) did a nice job of removing the Medieval Warm Period from their data, but not from the scientific literature-at-large. There are simply too many scientists reporting that the warming a thousand years ago was not only greater than our modern warming, but evident in locations all over the globe.

James Corbett, in his video report, "The IPCC Exposed," pointed to the criminal nature of Phil Jones's actions: "One of the interesting aspects of 'climate gate' that the people who want to sweep that entire scandal under the rug fail to ever point out is that the UK's information commissioner in fact found that Phil Jones and the other researchers at the... climatic research unit at the university of East Anglia actually did break the law by illegally withholding information from legitimate freedom of information requests that had been filed with the CRU. So, they were in fact found guilty of breaking the law, but was *[sic]* not prosecuted because by the time the information commissioner had received that complaint and the details of it, by the climate gate scandal, it was already past the statute of limitations for prosecution" (Corbett Report, 2013:0927).

Medieval Warm Period Persistence

In their original report, the IPCC used a graph which showed the Medieval Warm Period (MWP) as a camel-like hump somewhat larger than the recent, modern warming. This must not have been what the politicians wanted. When Michael Mann created his graph, the IPCC displayed it a number of times, even in color. His revision of history showed no more Medieval Warm Period and showed the Modern Warming Period as a skyrocketing trend at the end of an otherwise relatively flat graph. The shape was very much like that of a hockey stick.

Independent researchers had discovered that Mann's graph had been cobbled together with dissimilar kinds of data in order to achieve the desired shape. Getting rid of the Medieval Warm Period seemed to be a high priority.

In the meantime, other scientists have been busy investigating climate proxies in various parts of the world, discovering that the Medieval Warm Period did indeed exist and was global.

In a 2013 article, Anthony Watts provides nearly two dozen sources showing that the MWP was evident on the Antarctic Peninsula. Others found evidence in the South Shetland Islands, southern South America, the Scott Coast of Antarctica, the McMurdo Dry Valleys of Antarctica, the Drake Passage, Signey Island (near the Antarctic Peninsula), King George Island, Wilson Piedmont Glacier, Amery Ice Shelf and Tierra del Fuego

Some of the studies even included climate history going back two thousand years, showing that the Roman Warm Period was also global in scope (Watts, 2013:0411).

Sebastian Lüning, writing for Anthony Watts blog provides evidence from all over Australia and New Zealand of the MWP.

So, Michael Mann's attempts and those of other scientists, to make the Medieval Warm Period disappear have not worked. Their attempts to rewrite history have failed.

Rockefeller Front Man, Maurice Strong

How did we ever get to this point? Who started this wild ride into oblivion? Would it surprise you to know that biggest oil Rockefellers were behind the climate change scam? Their front man in all this was the late Maurice Strong—a high school dropout who happened to hobnob with the Rockefellers and other globalist royalty at an early age. With Rockefeller help, Strong became an oil multi-millionaire by his late 20s.

In 1969, the Swedish UN ambassador contacted Maurice Strong and asked if he'd be interested in heading up the UN's Conference on the Human Environment. With the help of the Rockefeller Foundation, Carnegie Fellow Barbara Ward, and Rockefeller ecologist Rene Dubos, Strong created the foundation of environmental thought and sustainable development. His Stockholm summit in 1972 has become the launch platform for Europe's governmentally-administered environmental action plans, and the United Nations Environment Program (UNEP), with Strong as its founding director.

After the 70s oil embargo crippled Canada's energy industry, government owned Petro-Canada was created with Strong as its first president. In 1987, Strong was one of the attendees at the Fourth World Wilderness Congress, also attended by David Rockefeller, James Baker and Edmund de Rothschild.

In 1992, Strong presided over the UN's Rio "Earth Summit." At that conference, the UN's Agenda 21 was born. From this was spawned the World Conservation Bank, and the World Bank funded "Global Environment Facility." This paved the way for the UN's Framework Convention on Climate Change (UNFCCC), the governing body which directs the Intergovernmental Panel on Climate Change (IPCC) (Corbett, 2016:0131).

In chapter 12, we will look at some possible reasons why the Rockefellers and their minions would do something like this. In the meantime, our next chapter looks at the effects climate and energy policies are having on Africa and America.

Chapter 7: Death of the African Dream; Death of the American Dream

"Tonight's forecast: Dark. Continued dark tonight, turning to partly light in the morning."—George Carlin, "George Carlin Again," 1978

The use of cheap, efficient energy has improved living conditions across much of the planet, especially in the developed nations. The use of fossil fuel energy in generating electricity has made it possible to cook meals without suffering from smoke inhalation. And no more suffering from undercooked meals that could threaten health. Refrigeration has allowed for the storage of food for longer periods of time. Of course, some of the "science experiments" I've discovered in refrigerators at work make me question the desirability of such things. But reduction in food spoilage has greatly increased the health of people all across America, Western Europe and other industrialized nations.

Clean water is another essential ingredient of modern civilization, made feasible in part from the use of easily accessible energy. Clean water makes it possible to practice good hygiene. Access to safe drinking water is also important. Modern energy, led by efficient fossil fuels has made these things far more achievable. Disease rates have plummeted in modern times in part because of this.

Human nature is so fascinating, though. I remember reading how one doctor who recommended that surgeons wash their hands before surgery had been ridiculed for such a "crank" idea. Boy, how times and understandings change. Perhaps one day doctors will realize that a major cause of disease may be related to what people actually put in their bodies on a daily basis. For veterinarians, this is obvious. Perhaps they're smarter than medical doctors.

How many people in Africa live without electricity, running water or sufficient food? Finding statistics on these is not easy. But some statistics might be a good indicator for these. The CIA database includes poverty levels in most nations of the world. Africa appears to be harder hit than all other continents put together.

The warming alarmists are fond of saying that it does no harm to be on the safe side by cutting back on the use of fossil fuels. But is this true?

In a British television documentary, *The Great Global Warming Swindle,* Paul Driessen, author of *Green Power, Black Death,* said, "My big concern with global warming is that the policies being pushed to supposedly prevent global warming are having a disastrous effect on the world's poorest people."

Driessen continued, "The precautionary principle is a very interesting beast. It's basically used to promote a particular agenda and ideology. It's always used in one direction only. It talks about the risks of using a particular technology—fossil fuels, for example—but never about the risks of not using it. It never talks about the benefits of having that technology" (British Channel 4).

A third of the world's population do not have access to electricity. This includes a large percentage of the people living in Africa.

According to the World Health Organization, 4 million children under the age of 5 die each year from respiratory ailments caused by the indoor smoke used for cooking. Many women die early from the same cause.

Without electricity, people have to go to sleep earlier and sleep longer. Without light, it's difficult to get anything done. Lack of refrigeration means food cannot be kept. The fires in most poor homes are too smoky to be used for heating. Accordingly, hot water remains either a luxury or non-existent.

Life expectancy in sub-Saharan Africa is the lowest of any region on the planet—60.6 years average. The healthiest continental African, sub-Saharan nation is Senegal at 66.7 years life expectancy. The best in the world is Japan at 83.7 years of average life expectancy. Ironically, the United States is number 31, at 79.3 years—behind South Korea, Canada, Greece, Slovenia, Cyprus and Costa Rica. Why this is so remains an entirely separate scandal of its own. The bottom 35 nations are all sub-Saharan Africa except Papua New Guinea and Afghanistan. Even as rich as is Nigeria with oil, life expectancy there is seventh from the bottom for the nations of the world. Something is terribly wrong about this picture.

"Evil" Industry Ordered to Cut Back on Energy Usage

All of the talk of evil carbon dioxide, because warming will supposedly destroy the planet, has led to politicians considering the idea of forcing corporations to cut back on their energy use.

Corporations have done some despicable things in the past, and likely continue to do so today. Corporate officers have a fiduciary responsibility to be selfish and to enlarge the bottom line. Would they kill to achieve that aim? Have they already? With corporations paying hundreds of millions of dollars in fines, or even billions, for fraud and endangerment to health, and for shoddy products rushed to market and the like, it should be clear to any sane individual that the system is broken. The system favors those with the money and influence. In a more perfect world, any corporate officer who jeopardizes the lives of millions with dangerous products should personally be held accountable. So should the stockholders. This might force those with the money to do far more due diligence before investing their money. When a corporation's actions lead to the deaths of thousands, and the maiming of millions, every corporate executive who had anything to do with that product should serve time in jail for at least negligent homicide and reckless endangerment.

What good are laws if they don't apply to all?

Africans Forced to Endure Deadly Poverty

Many Africans don't have enough food, too little fresh water (if any), and poor living conditions. Not everyone wants to live like an American. As an American, I don't. I used to, but not anymore. But there are certain minimum needs that are not being met for millions of people—not just Africa. But we will look at Africa as an example of a far larger problem.

Africans are being denied fossil fuel use because "the world" is cutting back on "carbon pollution." Africans are being told, "No, sorry. You're too late. Developing into First World nation status is no longer an option. We've ruined the environment and can't allow you to do the same."

Ironically, they're talking about the fake problem duo— "carbon pollution" and "global warming." No longer are they talking about real pollution, which is still a burgeoning problem they don't want to talk about. Corporations now have a gimmick to control others through carbon dioxide, but blithely forget to talk about the real pollution of toxic chemicals dumped all over the world. Ironically, corporations are being made out to be faux victims.

Most of the nations in Africa have 41–80% of their population living on less $1.25 per day. That's a stronger poverty signal than any other region of the planet. Nigeria is doing better than average with 6–20% of its population living on less than $1.25 per day.

But poverty is a bit more complicated than merely drawing a line at a specific dollar figure. Local economies allow people to eat for less, greatly reducing the cost of living. A meal for a family of four might cost $10 in one of the developed nations. In one of the poorer nations, a meal for a family of four might cost $1 or even less. In Haiti, small cakes made of real mud cost a few pennies. Yes, in some locations people are forced to eat dirt.

Each nation sets its own parameters for poverty levels. Though Nigeria is faring better than most of its neighbors for the $1.25 threshold, their definition of poverty sets the bar far higher than their neighbors. According to the CIA World Factbook (2008), more than 60% of Nigerians live in poverty.

By comparison with Nigeria, Mali has a far higher percentage of people living on less than $1.25 per day (41–60%), but Mali's definition of poverty has set the bar far lower so that only 30–40% of their population are considered to be living in poverty.

So, the definition of poverty is not as neat and tidy as we might hope.

Polluting the World for Profit

Corporations are notorious for dumping poisons into the environment. For instance, Monsanto's toxic glyphosate herbicide, RoundUp, is carcinogenic, according to the World Health Organization, and the poisons are ruining the soils of farmlands worldwide. Those same toxins are invading every nook and cranny of the ecosystem, even in human mother's milk.

Syngenta's atrazine is disrupting the biology of amphibians. And when the scientist they had hired—Tyrone Hayes—couldn't be bought off, they conspired to have him ruined. Corporations seem to take the notion of selfishness to new depths of depravity.

When corporations, like Monsanto, sell nations on the idea of better crop yields (a lie), they don't make it clear up front that buying Monsanto's GMO crops is tantamount to enslavement. No longer can farmers save seed to plant the following season. They have to buy new seed from Monsanto every season. That's not the only problem with Monsanto's artificial food. Crop yields seem to diminish every season because Monsanto's harsh chemicals are destroying the productivity of the soil. And the dream of perfect herbicides and pesticides has not yet been realized. Weeds are now RoundUp resistant, requiring far more of the herbicide in a never-ending downward spiral of greater and greater costs to keep the Monsanto myth afloat.

Solar and Wind—Nice Pipe Dreams

Solar energy has always been a sexy idea. But the efficiency of solar is still pretty low, and the cost per kilowatt-hour remains too high for most Africans to afford. For that matter, without government subsidies, solar would be too expensive for most Americans, too. Solar only works when the sun is shining.

During cloudy days and night time, solar panels are worthless. And solar doesn't deliver energy like fossil fuels. You need to cover a very large area to get sufficient energy to take care of basic needs.

How many Africans are dying because of a lack of potable water? How many are dying from a lack of sufficient energy. The figures quoted may be inflated on both sides of the climate debate. But it should be non-controversial to claim that energy is required to improve health and core living standards.

Those who cry about overpopulation don't know what they're talking about. Some enterprising individuals have figured out ways to produce lots of food in a small area making it feasible to have a human population on Earth in the hundreds of billions. So, food is not a problem. Greed and a lack of compassion are the problems. But the overpopulation meme is wrong on another level. It seems that population in any region tends to stabilize when prosperity is reached. The way to cure the pressures of population is to have everyone achieve prosperity.

It seems there are some self-proclaimed "elite" who don't like the idea of everyone becoming "special." And that's their own selfishness talking.

America Forced to Join Africans in Poverty

Those in America—supposedly the world's richest and most powerful nation—are slowly being forced to give up fossil fuels. This is disruptive at the very least. It could prove deadly to some who depend on cheap energy to survive. In Phoenix, Arizona, the heat can be a killer during summer. Without air conditioning, the heat can be brutal. I know. I lived there for ten years.

Living in cold climates during the winter can also prove to be deadly without cheap fossil fuels. Staying alive when the temperature drops below zero requires heating. If people cannot afford to heat their homes, the risk of death from the cold skyrockets.

The American government is attempting to make it more difficult for businesses to use fossil fuels. Tricky Biggest Oil Rockefellers have divested their portfolios of fossil fuel investments. It looked a bit hypocritical for them to be promoting a fear of warming while owning big oil stocks. They needed to keep up the illusion that fossil fuels are the cause of dangerous global warming.

With America's debt well over 18 Trillion dollars as this book is being written (nearly 4 times what it was before 9/11), crippling businesses with Draconian energy policies is certain to send the American economy into a tailspin that could trigger the Debt Balloon into popping. And that could make Americans vulnerable to the next stage of enslavement. From the standpoint of the self-proclaimed "elite" of the world, this would be a good thing, bringing them several steps closer to world domination. You have to love their cleverness on a project this big. Many of the clues to their purpose are sitting right out in the open, but people, in general, merely don't see it. Their eyes are glazed over by "American exceptionalism" and similar myths that "everybody knows."

When America's Debt Bubble pops, the entire world will be hard hit. People will scream for a solution, and the ones suppressing Africa's chances at First World status will have a "solution" waiting for us. How nice of them. Too bad that solution includes the deaths of millions, if not billions.

Chapter 8: The Real Culprit Behind Climate Change

"It's so dry the trees are bribing the dogs."—*Charles Martin,* Chasing Fireflies

What controls the climate? Of course, there are many factors, but CO_2 is one of the minor ones. The major culprits have nothing to do with humans and their machines. How do we know this? As we've already seen, the correlation between CO_2 and global average temperature doesn't exist, except that temperature drives carbon dioxide on the scale of hundreds to tens of thousands of years. Temperature has kept going up *and* down, while short-term carbon dioxide has kept going up. And naturally, warming is not the problem the United Nations makes it out to be. Someone wants to ruin economies in order to gain more political control. What they're doing is clever, but highly unethical—and dangerous.

One of a Series of Warm Periods

Did you know that there was a warm period that ended about 1100 BC. In fact, there have been ten distinct warm periods each about every thousand years ever since the Holocene interglacial began.

The repetitive nature of these warm periods shows that the Modern Warm Period is not unusual and likely not caused by humans. Whatever process caused the previous nine warm periods could have suddenly stopped just in time for humlans to take over, but that's not very likely.

The sun rises every day by nature. To take one day and declare that humans are the cause is the same kind of special lunacy.

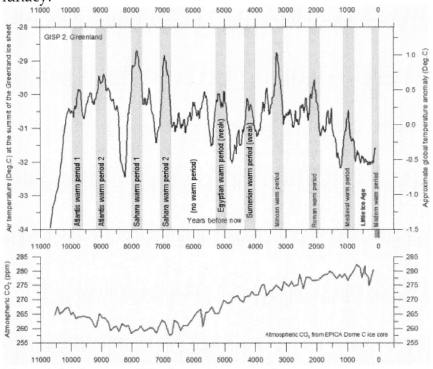

The original, unmodified graph comes from, http://climate4you.com/images/GISP2%20TemperatureSince107 00%20BP%20with%20CO2%20from%20EPICA%20DomeC.gif

That was for the last 10,700 years. Now, let's look at the last 450,000 years. The following graph by Ole Humlum,

University of Oslo, shows the semi-regular appearance of interglacials amongst the far deeper troughs of glacial cold. The brief periods of warmth, like our current Holocene, appear like the peaks of mountains overlooking broad valleys. The red box on the far right indicates the current, Holocene interglacial.

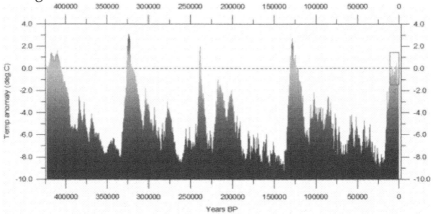

The space we're talking about here is time and temperature. Something is controlling the cycles of brief warming and prolonged cold. One of the natural forcings is the solar wind. A batch of natural forcings are related to the Earth's movement—rotation, orbital eccentricity, orbital tilt, position of aphelion and perihelion (farthest and closest points to the sun in its orbit), and several others.

It's on a scale similar to this that the levels of carbon dioxide and temperature seem to have the strongest correlation. But, as we've already seen, temperature comes first, then the increases in CO_2 from the ocean outgassing.

CO_2 Sensitivity

Imagine, for a moment, that you work in an office with one other person. Say that you don't really care what the thermostat is set at, no matter how cold it gets outside, you don't need to turn up the heat. We might say that you are "insensitive" to the cold. But let us say that your office mate is extremely sensitive. Every time they feel the slightest breeze, they have to jump up to adjust the thermostat a tad warmer.

From climate science, we know that carbon dioxide is a greenhouse gas. This merely means that it lets visible light through, but traps heat or infrared. When visible light strikes the surface of the Earth, especially if that surface is some color or black, that surface will convert the light into heat and re-radiate the energy back out. CO_2 won't let infrared out. Carbon dioxide molecules are not perfect border guards, but they do catch a large percentage of their infrared escapees.

What scientists have been arguing about is how sensitive carbon dioxide is to turning up the thermostat. If we doubled the border patrol, would they force the thermostat of Earth up by 1 °C or 5 °C? Or something in between?

If the sensitivity is high enough, we would have dangerous, runaway greenhouse warming that would boil the oceans and cook the planet, turning Earth into a hotbox like Venus. If the sensitivity is slightly less, we might have dangerous spikes in temperature forced on us by carbon dioxide. But if the sensitivity is low, then the climate would remain relatively stable with no danger from catastrophic warming despite higher and higher levels of CO_2.

One reason we know the sensitivity is low is from the paleoclimatic history of Earth. Carbon dioxide levels of the past 600 million years have been as high as 4,000 parts-per-million, and possibly higher. That's ten times our current scare. Earth did not burn up. In fact, it appears that something else was controlling the temperature. When the Earth warmed up, more carbon dioxide was forced out of the ocean's dissolved reservoir of CO_2 gas. But the extra CO_2 did not accelerate the process.

The Water Switch—Controlling the Climate

Unlike other planets, Earth has a fancy, automatic thermostat to help control the climate. If it gets too warm, water cools it down. If it gets too cool, water helps to warm things up. It's not perfect, but it has kept the average global temperature of our planet within an extremely narrow range of temperatures. When you use the absolute temperature scale of degrees Kelvin (same units as Celsius, but a different zero position), the hottest and coldest periods of Earth's history show a range of only about 5% variation over the last 600 million years. That's amazingly steady.

The Real Culprit: The Sun

What really controls Earth's climate? If you were hoping for something controversial or shocking, let me apologize up front. The answer is pretty simple and very plain. It's the sun. Imagine that.

If the sun were suddenly to go out as if someone threw a power switch and shut it off, Earth would plummet into a deep freeze. All life would die as temperatures quickly descended toward absolute zero.

Quite the opposite is happening, though, and far more slowly. Our sun is gradually warming up and has been ever since it was first delivered into the main sequence some four and a half billion years ago. In several hundred million years, the sun will be sufficiently brighter to make life on the surface of Earth difficult, if not impossible to survive. But this warming is so incredibly slow, it has absolutely nothing to do with our current warming and cooling cycles.

Svensmark study

The beautiful thing about real science is that there is always something more to learn. When I first heard about Henrik Svensmark and his research on cloud formation, I felt immediately encouraged that he and his team were onto something remarkable.

The sun's light has remained amazingly steady for billions of years. As we've mentioned, the amount of light has been slowly increasing throughout the sun's life, but this is too slow a process to be controlling the shorter period fluctuations in climate. Instead, we look to the other major output of the sun—solar wind. This fluctuates greatly over an eleven year cycle, and these fluctuations also change over a longer period of time. The solar wind maximum every eleven years also goes up and down. Solar wind strength seems to be partially correlated to the number of sunspots. More spots, more solar wind. During the Little Ice Age, the sun spot maximum nearly disappeared down to zero. This meant very little solar wind. When that happens, cosmic rays from elsewhere in the galaxy have an easier time invading the Solar system and bombarding the atmosphere of Earth.

What Svensmark and his team investigated was the notion that more cosmic rays means more clouds. Like a hydrogen bubble chamber, the fast particles of nuclear radiation leave bubble trails that can be likened to the formation of cloud droplets. When there are more clouds, less sunlight can get to the surface, and the planet as a whole becomes cooler. This seems to explain very well what happened during the Little Ice Age. Early astronomers noticed sunspots nearly disappear and the Earth was plunged into a period of cold and stormy climate.

Right now, the sun is headed for another sunspot minimum. Some scientists are concerned that we could be headed for another Little Ice Age. That could be devastating enough to the worldwide economy, and to crop yields. Millions could starve.

But we don't yet know what causes interglacial periods to end. The Milankovitch cycles of varying solar input caused by orbital changes, tilt in the Earth's axis and similar factors would certainly play a part. Svensmark's cloud factor would also play a part. But are there any other factors? We still don't know enough.

The fact that our current interglacial is overdue to end should concern everyone. The Holocene is 11,500–17,000 years old, and the average interglacial is 11,000 years long, according to W.S. Broecker (1998). At the very least, we should be thinking about what we can do to prepare for the cold so that starvation is minimized.

We should also consider the possibility that we might be able to end the current Ice Age. We will look more closely at this idea in "Part 3: The Cure."

Part 2: Cryophilia

cryophilia *n.* — An attraction to or preference for cold (*cryo-*, cold, freezing; *-philia*, attraction to or preference for)

Chapter 9: End of the Holocene

"We can, of course, be deceived in many ways. We can be deceived by believing what is untrue, but we certainly are also deceived by not believing what is true."—*Søren Kierkegaard,* Works of Love, *1847*

When you live in an Ice Age interglacial, the inevitable end to that interglacial will bring with it all manner of regrets. Why? Because people really do prefer the warmth. The idea of perpetual winter is anathema to life itself. Those who promote a fear of warmth—thermophobia—are implying a love of the cold—cryophilia.

The average length of an interglacial in the current Ice Age stands at about 11,000 years. According to W.S. Broecker (1998), the Holocene is between 11,500 and 17,000 years old, depending on the definitions used. This means that the Holocene is already 500–6,000 years overdue to end.

Nature is notoriously complex and messy. It's not a metal machine with precision timing. It works on a near-infinite number of inputs. There is some repetition, but it's rather fuzzy around the edges. Interglacials have happened almost like clockwork roughly every 100,000 years. Interglacials have ranged from 4,000 years in length up to 28,000 years. Of the 9 most recent interglacials, only 4 of them were longer than our current interglacial. From the present going back, the Eemian was 18,000 years long, then 4,000 years, 14,000 years, 28,000 years, 14,000 years, 9,000 years, 6,000 years, and 5,000 years. The oldest 4 of this batch were relatively weak (cool), compared to the most recent 5.

Glacial periods were as short as 28,000 years and as long as 143,000 years. So, nature is not a perfect timepiece. Still, the 100,000-year average has remained fairly steady for the last one million years.

For the 1.6 million years prior to that, our current Ice Age had a 41,000-year average cycle. Why the switch? That remains one of the unsettled mysteries of climate science. It likely has something to do with Milankovitch cycles—various parameters of Earth's orbit, rotation and Solar system passage through the galaxy. But Milankovitch cycles are not the only factors to be considered. We saw what are the real culprits behind climate change in the last chapter, but more study is needed to know all of the players with greater certainty. We want to know how much each member participates.

What a Glacial Period is Like

In the next chapter, we will take a closer look at the implications of the Holocene interglacial period ending. We will look at the negative side, where those two little white things at the poles persist and grow much, much larger.

Chapter 10: Ninety Thousand Years of Ice

"The frost performs its secret ministry, Unhelped by any wind." —
Samuel Taylor Coleridge, *"Frost at Midnight"*

A glacial period of the current Ice Age is merely more of the same cold which currently grips the poles in deadly ice. It should be obvious to any human who has experienced such cold that it kills. But the cold is not the only problem.

Colder climate brings with it cooler oceans. That means less evaporation and less water vapor in the air. This translates to fewer clouds, less rain, larger deserts, more droughts and more dust in the air.

Colder climate also brings with it a greater frequency of storms and more violent storms. This is because polar cold moves closer to equatorial heat. This creates a far greater thermal potential—the basis for violent storms.

During the last glacial period, deserts were far larger, because rainfall was far more scarce. This meant that life was more scarce. Human population was likely well below 100,000. Food was more scarce, too. Because of the lack of rain, agriculture was not something humans could easily start. Even irrigation farming requires rain somewhere.

Effects of Another Glacial Period on Civilization

After several thousand years of global warming, civilization was able to start about 12,000 years ago. If we lose our foothold on warmth, how much of civilization would we lose?

The technology might persist, but the infrastructure for mass market manufacturing will likely disappear. Canada and up to a third of the United States will become buried in a permanent layer of snow that will gradually become deeper and deeper over the years. Snowfall will slow considerably, but it will continue, building the layer of ice from several inches, to several feet, then dozens of feet. Eventually, it may again become a mile thick toward the interior.

Not only does North America lose a great deal of its farm land from the snow, but it will also lose much more farm land from the lack of rain and from the persistent cold coming off of the permanent snow pack.

With sources of food hard hit, population levels will plummet as millions of people starve to death. With technological infrastructure gone, basic services such as clean water and sanitation will disappear in many regions, leading to the spread of diseases. Because people are basically selfish and self-concerned, food wars will likely result in more deaths as people scramble to secure the sustenance they require in order to survive.

How many people can Earth support during a glacial period? That is uncertain. But one thing remains clear. Without adequate preparation, billions could die.

The notion of stopping any and all "climate change" is perhaps noble, but naive. You cannot stop the wind. But we can prepare for the changes that do happen.

It seems that some have already started preparations, but they have left most of us to dangle out in the cold.

The Tropics

These will remain largely unchanged, except for a likely increase in violent storms.

The Deserts

The desert regions will grow in size, spreading out like a disease.

The Temperate Zones

Temperate regions will shrink in size, squeezed between the zones of glaciation and the deserts. Tornadoes will become more common and stronger.

The Frozen Zones

Regions of permanent glaciation will become far larger, especially where land resides close to polar regions and sources of water vapor for precipitation. This will include North America and Northern Europe.

An "Ark" in Arkansas for the Self-Proclaimed "Elite?"

An underground bunker has been built, possibly at taxpayer expense, in Arkansas. The underground facility is huge, but was unguarded when Jesse Ventura and his film crew decided to investigate (*Conspiracy Theory*, season 3, episode 7). In the Ozarks region, this bunker appears to be large enough to sustain a population of several thousand for years. And there may be more than one bunker.

David Rockefeller, in his *Memoirs,* confessed to having conspired for years against the best interests of the United States. His goals involve the establishment of a one-world government. And because the Rockefeller family has long supported eugenics, they likely don't want most of us to be around when they take over.

Chapter 11: Geoengineering

"When I feel like exercising, I just lie down until the feeling goes away." — Paul Terry, June 13, 1937

When I read about the global warming and climate change problems we have, it reminds me of the satire of Jonathan Swift—about the "important" debate concerning which end of the egg should be opened—the debate between Big-Endians and Little-Endians. Both sides are fighting over whether or not warming is currently happening; but they're missing the fact that we reside in an Ice Age. Such shortsightedness misses the bigger picture—that such trivial things are decidedly unimportant.

When complex plans are developed for combating global warming, it's ironically like Gulliver's little friends if they were to declare that there was too much food in the world. Tax the farmers for growing crops so they'll eventually have to stop. Sew the mouths of consumers shut so they will no longer demand food. And belts make it obvious when people are hungry, because those people have to tighten them to keep up their pants. So, outlaw belts, too. See? Wrong focus.

Wrong set of importances. Wrong problem! Food is not the problem and neither is warming.

We can become entirely too creative with this climate madness once we accept the original lie that warmth is bad. Then, if we accept the next lie, that human creation of carbon dioxide is the cause for more "evil" warmth, then we can outlaw the use of fossil fuels, destroying civilization in the process. And to think that the Lilliputians went to war over breakfast manners.

How could eliminating fossil fuels destroy civilization? Without an adequate replacement, people could freeze in the winter (those who live in the land of snow). People who live in the desert southwest could die from the heat and lack of water. Transporting water to the desert takes energy. So does running air-conditioning to ward off the extreme desert heat. When energy becomes too expensive, people and companies die. And with the United States debt climbing above $18 trillion, it's only a matter of time before the pressures of mismanagement and Draconian economic policies bankrupt America.

Combating global warming is like combating too much food or too much prosperity.

So, it becomes doubly ironic when governments develop plans to tax global warming out of existence and to seed the skies with blankets of whiteness to shut out the sun, like those clouds after a volcanic eruption. CIA director, John Brennan, gushed about this wonderful approach in a speech at the Council on Foreign Relations on June 29, 2016. Is Brennan stupid? Does he not know that volcanic eruptions have disrupted agriculture, causing famines? I suspect that he's not stupid; that only leaves "corrupt." Why else would someone promote a tactic that would result in the deaths of millions?

Tic-Tac-Toe in the Sky

In 1953, I saw my first jet airplane. It was an almost imperceptible dot reflecting the light of the West Texas sun over my head. I remember the trail behind it disappearing within a second or two. For the next 44 years, this was my view of jet aircraft condensation trails (contrails). They were short-lived. They did not disrupt my appreciation of the skies. Ever!

I'm a space fanatic. I love wide open spaces. I love the broad, clean skies of Earth. My soul lifts up to meet all that space and fills it with appreciation. I've been an avid, amateur astronomer since the mid-50s.

In 1997, this all changed. It started slowly, at first. That year, I moved to Phoenix, Arizona to work for my brother in his manufacturing facility. That year, I noticed jet condensation persist for the first time. I thought it was odd, but didn't give it much thought. I had only recently moved to a new city. My mind justified the difference as a product of my new environment.

Over the next four years, the persistence of jet condensation trails waxed and waned. I grew increasingly annoyed at the phenomenon. By 2002, my blood started a slow boil as my skies were now a patchwork of lines crisscrossing from one horizon to the other. These trails persisted for hours— sometimes for the entire day. Something was definitely wrong. Had technology changed? Were jet aircraft using a new type of engine? Certainly, air traffic had not increased significantly from 1996 to 2002.

In 2007, I moved to the Philippines. I was happy to have clean skies once again, devoid of the crisscrossing lines of some giant's tic-tac-toe game. I left all that behind in Phoenix.

But last November (2015), I noticed a short stretch of persistent jet trail. It stopped for several hundred feet, and picked up again, starting, stopping and starting again a couple of times. Just like the first few years of this phenomenon in Arizona, the "disease" had found its way to the Philippines. Now, almost daily, I notice evidence of short stretches of persistent trails, blown by the tropical winds. They are not natural clouds. On occasion, I notice what looks like particulates dropping out from the trail, like precipitates in a chemical experiment.

What's going on?

Weather Control and Global Warming Abatement

Humans have attempted to control the weather from at least the 1960s, and possibly earlier. Cloud seeding has been used to cause more rain. Papers have been written promoting the idea of upper atmosphere spraying to reflect sunlight in order to help cool down the planet. Cooling in an ongoing Ice Age? That's like rescuing a man suffering from hypothermia and drenching him with a bucket of ice water to cool off. In case you don't know, hypothermia is a condition when the body's core temperature drops below 95 °F (35 °C)—dangerously cold. Dunking someone in ice water who is suffering hypothermia is both stupid and criminal. Doing the same on a planetary scale is genocidal.

As thoroughly insane as governments have been in the past, it wouldn't surprise me if the persistent contrails I've seen since 1997 were part of an ongoing attempt to modify the Earth's climate—a campaign about which no one thought to warn us. Cooling the Earth in an ongoing Ice Age? Lunacy! But scientists, politicians and even the CIA director are talking about it. The emperor's new clothes are wonderful, aren't they?

Too bad they're all a lie. Too bad the benign helpfulness of the psychopaths in government is all a sham. What are they really doing?

As we will see in the next chapter, we don't know for certain what their end game is, but we have sufficient clues to remain concerned.

Chapter 12: Why?

"There is no right way of doing a wrong thing; and while the relation itself is allowed to continue, the mode of acting under that relation must partake of its vicious and unnatural character." — W. Adam, De Bow's Southern and Western Review, *July 1850*

Why would anyone promote global cooling in an Ice Age? Why would anyone kidnap a scientific term and replace it with a shallow imposter? When people tell lies, they're usually hiding something. Not always, but usually. I knew a woman from Thailand who lied regularly. Quite often, she lied just to stay in practice—to keep her mind sharp. I thought that was curious behavior. At least that's what she told me. Perhaps that was a lie, too.

Sometimes people tell lies to protect others. That can be good, sometimes, but it can create unforeseen problems.

We've already looked at the fact that people are inherently selfish and self-concerned. I used to think that people are inherently good, but it seems that they merely and only have that potential. First, they have to choose to be good. When pushed into a corner, most people—perhaps more than

99%—would choose the selfish path. We have to understand this fact if we are to deal with its consequences.

Because people are basically selfish, conspiracies are dirt ordinary. I fact, there are at least 489 new conspiracies starting every second somewhere in the world, on average, day-in and day-out, every day and all year long. And this is only the count based on documented conspiracies. Because criminals like to remain anonymous, this number is likely somewhat higher (Martin).

Even though people are inherently selfish, I remain optimistic. People can choose not to be selfish. They are not permanently tied down by their egos. They can escape their evil side.

The most psychopathic people in the world clamor for wealth and power. Without these, they feel vulnerable. They know the difference between right and wrong, but don't care. They look at the world as their own playground. Everyone else is merely an obstacle which needs to be removed.

As an enterprising group, they have learned to use human nature—selfishness—to an extreme advantage. They know how to create problems which elicit fear, and then to supply solutions to that fear and the problems which created it. Bankers in the early 1900s created a rumor which led to a bank run. It destroyed some banks, ruined fortunes and made the public-at-large fearful of banks. Then, those bankers and fellow conspirators, created a plan which would give them power over all banks and the American economy. They had their puppets in government attack the bankers so people would trust them. And then they had legislation passed which was said to put bankers in their place. In reality, it allowed bankers to stage a financial coup for taking over the govern-ment. And it worked. Carefully, they chose the name of this instrument of enslavement. They called it "federal" so that people would think it was part of the government. They called it a "reserve" so that it would sound safe and secure. And they called it a "system," instead of a loathsome bank, so people would trust it. Thus, the Federal Reserve System, or "Fed," was born in 1913. This was the same year the personal income tax was started. Before then, the government ran perfectly well without those taxes. But now, American citizens were paying for their own enslavement (Griffin).

The Fed was said to be necessary to reduce the dangers of depressions and recessions. Yet, when the Great Depression started, the Fed tightened money, instead of loosening it. Businesses needed liquidity to help them pull out of the depression. Loosening their grip on money was what was needed. The Fed's actions only deepened the Depression. Why? To gain more power—more control over the nation and its government.

The Fed is owned by its member banks. And the member banks are owned by private individuals. So, the Federal Reserve System is as much a part of the government as Federal Express delivery service, or McDonalds hamburger restaurant chain.

Rockefeller Wet Dream

In order to take over the entire planet, people have to be willing to give up their power to the self-proclaimed "elite." Fear of bankers let bankers create the Fed in 1913. Fear of terrorism let psychopaths strip away the liberties of American citizens in 2001. Many Americans don't know the value of those liberties and how difficult they were to achieve in the first place, so they traded them for a false sense of security.

Benjamin Franklin, one of America's founding fathers, once wrote, "Those who would give up essential Liberty, to purchase a little temporary Safety, deserve neither Liberty nor

Safety" (Franklin's reply from the Pennsylvania Assembly to the Governor, 1755:1111). Franklin's wisdom comes back to haunt us in our time of fear and laziness. Lazy? If only more people studied history and understood how precious those liberties were. The freedoms protected by the American Constitution and Bill of Rights were entirely new on the world stage when they became the foundation for laws in the United States. Every law written since 9/11 which works against that foundation is basically illegal. What are citizens to do when there are two laws on the books which contradict each other?

The Rockefeller family has long used public relations to sell a positive image to the world-at-large. Beneath the veneer of respectability is a dark layer of corruption. Every move they've taken has been based on one selfish motive or another. Any apparent altruism was merely a front for one of their sinister agendas.

While pretending to care about the planet, they funded research into overpopulation. They supported Margaret Sanger and her views on eugenics—to weed out the undesirable types of humans by sterilization and other methods. They would likely feel quite different about eugenics if galactic conquerors came and found them to be inadequate and undeserving of survival. But we should not wish that inhumanity on anyone, including them.

The Centers for Disease Control (CDC) in America has a dark past (and present). They illegally experimented on American citizens, giving them diseases and then studying how they died. This unreal and obscene program continued into the 1970s (Brandt). This wasn't the only crime committed by the American government. Another batch of medical experiments was conducted in Guatemala, intentionally infecting people without their knowledge or consent. The study took place 1946–1948. In 2010, the US government apologized for their crimes (Bazell).

Years later, a CDC whistleblower came clean about lies told by CDC scientists and administrators about a link between the MMR vaccine and autism (Wakefield). This only accented the corrupt nature of government and its ties to selfish corporations and the self-proclaimed "elite" who own them.

In 2016, a film was released concerning the CDC's corruption and lies—*Vaxxed: From Cover-Up to Catastrophe*. The corporate media and even Wikipedia have created such a flurry of lies that any reasonable person would have a hard time discerning the truth. Wikipedia, for instance calls the film and its director "anti-vaccine," but Dr. Andrew Wakefield has made it clear on numerous occasions that he is not anti-vaccine; that he is merely calling for safer vaccines. Somehow the truth gets lost in the rush to protect profits and egos.

Del Bigtree, producer of the film said in an interview that many of the doctors he contacted while making the film were unwilling to be a part of the documentary. They said that they were well aware that there was a relationship between MMR vaccine and autism, but were afraid that their own careers would become ruined like that of Dr. Wakefield. They did not want to become "wakefielded."

America, with its freedoms, posed a grave threat to the plans of the powerful psychopaths. Gutting that nation of its freedoms was of utmost importance. But the psychopathic "elite" have been patient. They have worked for more than a century to erode the freedoms of America, building it up into a superpower, only to bring it down when the debt bubble pops.

The remainder of the world no longer trusts the now evil empire of America. Evil? Attacking one nation after another without provocation and based on fabricated intelligence? These are not the acts of a sane and honorable nation.

For decades, the American government has become increasingly infiltrated by corporate officers and lobbyists. For example, Monsanto's GMO crops rocketed through the approval process, because the agency executives used to work for that corporation. And when French scientists found GMOs to be deadly, Monsanto sent one of their executives into the scientific journal to become an editor and to have the pesky science article and one other critical of Monsanto, retracted. Clever, but a setback for honest science.

Getting rid of 7 billion people is not easy. With the current population of Earth at about 7.5 billion, eliminating 93% would leave about 500 million. This would be plenty of people to service the psychopaths in their wet dream of power and world domination.

Growing up, I used to love the idea of a united Earth. The Federation portrayed in the television series, *Star Trek*, seemed to be an ideal worth achieving. The problem with a one-world government is that tyranny, once established, would provide no possibility of escape. When tyranny reared its ugly head in places like Germany, before World War II, people fled. But when tyranny owns the entire planet, refugees have no destination.

Getting people to contribute to their own self-destruction is one of the master strokes of human history. Lies make such things possible. Getting people to think that warmth is dangerous would have them fear the one thing that could save them from another deadly glacial period.

Making that warming doubly evil by blaming it on wicked corporations would help to make the plan emotionally self-reinforcing. Conflating real pollution with beneficial CO_2

would also make it difficult for people to change their minds about "climate change."

Clever, but psychopathic. The kings of old were brave thieves and murderers. The Rockefellers, Rothschilds and their ilk have beautiful justifications in their own minds for murdering billions. It's for the victims' own good and for the good of the planet.

Part 3: The Cure

cure *n.*—Something that corrects or relieves a harmful or disturbing situation

Chapter 13: A Warm World

"The rain thundered down so heavily that Pritam could imagine that space itself was made of water and was pouring through rents in the sky's tired fabric."—Stephen M. Irwin, The Dead Path

What would a truly warm world look like? Scientists have sufficient data to give us an idea—a glimpse of what it would be like to live outside an Ice Age. And it sounds pretty nice—not perfect, but very, very nice.

Tropics

The tropics would remain relatively unchanged in a world without permanent polar ice. Perhaps the most significant change would be the reduction or complete loss of violent storms. Who would weep for that? With a much milder thermal gradient, the power pack which drives strong storms would be largely missing.

Desert Zones

Another scientific paper demonstrated that desert zones formed by Hadley cells will shift and shrink (Hasegawa).

During the far warmer Holocene Optimum—a global phenomenon—the Sahara Desert was green and today's wimpy Lake Chad rivaled the Caspian Sea in its heyday.

Temperate Regions

Temperate zones would be much larger and would not include the winter season. In fact, temperate climate would stretch virtually all the way to the poles. Depending on the resulting average global temperature, the poles may or may not experience snow during their winter seasons. This is when the region is in permanent darkness for three months. High latitude mountains will likely experience occasional snows during the cooler months of the year. Skiing fanatics might be able to indulge their pastime on the slopes.

Like the tropics, temperate zones will have far fewer violent storms, or none at all.

Frozen Zones

No place on Earth will be permanently cold, except the depths of the oceans, where it remains only slightly warmer than freezing.

Not Like Venus

Some uneducated warming alarmists have claimed that Earth is in danger of becoming like Venus—dry and too hot for life. Venus, however, has several factors working against it. Surface pressure on Earth's twin sister is a bone crushing 92 atmospheres. The composition by volume includes 96.5% carbon dioxide, compared to Earth's 0.04% CO_2. And Venus stands 28% closer to the sun. With the greater sunlight, and the thick blanket of greenhouse CO_2, Venus has a surface temperature of 462 °C—362 °C above the boiling point of water.

For Earth to become like Venus, it would have to bump its sister out of orbit and take its place. Earth would have to have nearly 100 times the atmospheric mass that it has now.

One factor that works in our favor is Earth's water surface—71%. Evaporation of water helps to regulate Earth's temperature so it can never reach a runaway state while our sun remains relatively constant in brightness. The oceans are thus not in danger of boiling away.

Let's be clear about our global warming: it's melting ice and *not* boiling water. That's a huge difference that some of our less intelligent fellow citizens don't seem to realize.

With the warmest we can expect being in the deserts, and those deserts being far smaller, life on Earth is allowed to thrive across a far wider range of latitudes.

Chapter 14: Awareness of the Lies and the Real Problems

"To be a teacher does not mean simply to affirm that such a thing is so, or to deliver a lecture, etc. No, to be a teacher in the right sense is to be a learner. Instruction begins when you, the teacher, learn from the learner, put yourself in his place so that you may understand what he understands and the way he understands it."—Søren Kierkegaard, The Point of View for My Work as an Author, *1848*

One of the key impediments to awareness is arrogance. This is the attitude of the person who thinks they know it all about a certain topic or field. In their own minds, they think their level of logic is superior to that of the average person. They've done all of the heavy lifting, studying the topic in-depth. Their view of the world is complete and they don't need to hear anything from anyone else. Differences in viewpoint are always the other person's delusion.

What makes this state of mind so troublesome is the fact that the person crippled by it, is never aware that they need to learn something more. They remain stuck on a plateau of knowledge and move no further. They don't see the path leading up to the next plateau.

The optimum state of mind is that of the humble and restrained, perpetual student. There is always more to learn. Every fact of knowledge may be wrong in some subtle or significant manner. For example, Sir Isaac Newton's "laws" of motion were found to be flawed in certain cases. Perhaps calling them "laws" was counterproductive. Einstein found a better way of stating the truth behind the effects of motion. Yet, despite his genius, he too became somewhat arrogant and dismissed the entire field of quantum mechanics. "As I have said so many times," Einstein told William Hermanns in 1943, "God doesn't play dice with the world." And if God does indeed play dice, then Einstein would have been keeping himself from that discovery.

Critical Thinking Skills

In any field, we need to sharpen our critical thinking skills. We need to recognize the patterns of logical fallacies so we can dismiss them when they occur, even within our own minds. We need to see the assumptions we and others make. Upon what facts do we rely? What if one of those facts is false?

Part of critical thinking is also the ability not to become entirely satisfied with our state of knowledge. We need to consider any knowledge as temporarily "workable" but potentially "imperfect."

Humility to Keep Researching Even When We Think We Have an Answer

We need to keep looking at our topic from various viewpoints. When we think we're done, we need to invent new viewpoints outside of those already considered.

This is part of the humility required to learn new things.

There is an old story of a monk and an aristocrat. The high-born official came to the monk and asked how he might find Truth. The monk invited him to sit for tea and poured for his guest. But he kept pouring and pouring. The cup overflowed and spilled tea all over the aristocrat's fine silk clothes.

"You idiot! Don't you see that my cup is already full?"

"Yes," replied the monk with the slightest hint of a smile. "Please come back when you have emptied your cup."

Of course, the monk was not talking about a literal cup of tea. He was talking about the aristocrat's attitude. The government official was not yet ready to learn anything, because his mind was too cluttered with fixed ideas and knowledge that would make it impossible for him to see, much less learn, the Truth he sought.

An empty cup is the humility to give up all that we know. The knowledge we once held is still there, but no longer attached to our ego.

This additional state, beyond critical thinking, is more art than science. It's a skill you only learn through passion, compassion and humility.

But with this skill, you can learn the secrets of the universe. This is the real paradigm underlying scientific discovery and, in fact, discovery of any kind.

Chapter 15: Prepare Humanity for the Cold (if necessary)

"In omnibus negotiis prius quam aggrediare, adhibenda est præparatio diligens." [In all matters, before beginning, a diligent preparation should be made.]—Cicero, De Officiis, 44 BC

We have two possible directions we can go which will secure the future for humanity. A third direction—ignorance—will lead to humanity's destruction.

One of the beneficial choices involves preparation. We need to prepare for the cold that will likely come our way. There may be low-cost preparations we can make, and we should certainly do these first.

More expensive preparations should at least be planned and the infrastructure put into place so that implementation can be made quickly once it is needed. This would include things like moving entire communities farther south, away from the new zones of permanent snow cover.

We need to establish likely zones of farming with the knowledge that rain will likely be scarce. Water is already a problem in most parts of the world, including America. Cities like Los Angeles and Phoenix depend on dwindling supplies and unpredictable sources. We need innovations in desalination techniques—turning the vast supply of sea water into fresh water. Such technology might even be useful when the Ice Age finally ends.

Agreements need to be hammered out so that Canadians can move to the United States when they lose their entire nation to permanent snow. Refugees from Scandinavia need similar arrangements in central and southern Europe. Russians need to plan for several million of their own to move south.

As an alternative, Canadians and northern Europeans may find ways to live in permanent ice while keeping some semblance of infrastructure—roads, water supplies, food storage and perhaps even some method of growing crops in the snow. As glaciers build up around them and start to move, northerners would need to keep those glaciers from destroying what infrastructure they have.

Because violent storms multiply during periods of increased glaciation, methods of building should to be developed which resist destruction from high winds. Some techniques already exist, but they need to be made more readily available where storms will be more common.

During the last glacial period, conditions were so poor, human population levels were suppressed to the tens of thousands. Technology may be able to help us get around those problems. The only real problem in our way is a lack of awareness and the willingness to use superior management skills to administer our resources. We also need to be aware of the fact that there are some unscrupulous individuals who would love to manage those same resources for their own selfish benefit, to the disadvantage of everyone else in our world.

Slowly, sea levels will drop. This might start more quickly and slow dramatically as oceans cool and snow becomes more scarce along with the rain. But snow in a permanently cold realm will accumulate, depriving that water from the oceans of the world. Many port cities will become useless as harbors of commerce, because ships will no longer be able to reach them. We need to have infrastructure that can move with the falling sea levels.

There may be other problems to address. This is something the entire world should be discussing and brainstorming.

No one knows when the next glacial period will begin. We still don't know enough about climate to predict such things. We do know, however, that we are near the peak of one of the once-in-a-1,000-year warm periods of the Holocene interglacial of the current Ice Age. We also know that our sun is going into sleep mode with sunspot maximums that are about the same as the minimums. This means that the solar wind will be weak to non-existent, allowing more cosmic rays to bombard Earth. With that, we will see more cloud formation and a massive cooling of the Earth. Will we move into another "Little Ice Age" like the one humanity experienced 400 years ago, or will this be the tipping point which will end the current interglacial and send us plummeting into the frozen abyss?

Are we now standing on the verge of another 90,000 years of immense glaciation? No one knows. But based on the average length of interglacials, we're currently overdue. The least we can do for ourselves and our children is to plan. We need to ask ourselves, "If the ice comes this afternoon, what do we need in order to survive and thrive?"

Chapter 16: End the Ice Age (if possible)

"Human knowledge and human power meet in one; for where the cause is not known the effect cannot be produced. Nature to be commanded must be obeyed..." — *Francis Bacon,* Novum Organum *(1620)*

We've seen one possible path toward survival. We need to prepare for the eventual cold, whether it comes later this afternoon, or holds off for several thousand years. Preparation means that nature cannot catch us off-guard. It means that we may be able to protect our hard-won asset: civilization, which was originally made possible by global warming.

Terraforming Earth

Terraforming is a concept which has long captured my imagination. In the 1970s, I acquired data on Mars from the USGS office in Flagstaff, Arizona. I brushed up on the mathematics of planetary atmospheres. I calculated what was required to make Mars more habitable, like Earth.

When the next glaciation starts, Earth will become far less habitable. So, the notion of terraforming (making like habitable Earth) our own world is not so farfetched.

Humans are capable of some remarkable achievements when they cooperate in striving toward a worthy goal.

In China, humans were forced to build a great wall which stretched for over thirteen thousand miles (more than twenty-one thousand kilometers). This included numerous branches, some running in parallel.

In Egypt, humans built massive pyramidal structures the likes of which the world has never seen since. Before the Egyptians, unknown cultures cut and moved far more massive stones in Lebanon and Peru—gargantuan blocks which likely would be beyond our own capabilities today.

In the 1960s, Americans prepared for and ultimately accomplished sending men to the Moon and returning them safely to our home planet.

Could we reclaim our world from the ice? Would protecting our future from colossal glaciation be a worthwhile aim?

Methods

How can we warm up the planet enough to melt the ice? Remember that warming goes mainly to the poles. Very little global warming goes to the equator. The notion that Earth will burn up is only a scare tactic with no basis in reality.

One method involves the simple idea of making ice dark so that it absorbs sunlight rather than reflects it. Could we spread black carbon over the snow to strategically slice off chunks of ice from Greenland and Antarctica?

One idea I remember from a magazine article in the 1970s involved towing large icebergs to desert regions and siphoning the ice water inland for farming and other uses.

Reservoirs could be built inland to hold vast amounts of fresh water in Africa, South America, the American Southwest and Australian interior.

We need to make certain that the black carbon particles don't end up disrupting life in the oceans.

Another idea involves manufacturing reusable, black panels which absorb and hold heat for melting glacial ice. Rather than spending trillions of dollars on carbon taxes, which end up only fattening the corrupt bankers, we could spend a few billion to manufacture black panels for strategic melting of polar glaciers.

Satellites can be built and placed in orbit which reflect large amounts of solar energy toward polar waters making them warmer.

We need to stop all of the geoengineering programs which are currently reflecting more sunlight away from the Earth. After all, warming is the solution; not the problem.

One other possible solution involves building a huge, underwater barrier in the southern ocean to block the circum-Antarctic current. This current is one factor which keeps the Antarctica glaciers cold. Millions of years ago, when tectonic plate movement took Australia away from Antarctica, permanent ice was able to form on the most southerly continent because Australia no longer blocked the current which now encircles Antarctica. This could be the most expensive project of those mentioned, but it could prove to be the simplest one for helping to ensure Antarctica does not freeze over again, after we're done melting all the ice.

Caveats

The largest problem from ending the current Ice Age would obviously be the rising sea levels. All that ice sitting above sea level, nestled on Greenland and Antarctica, would raise sea levels by about 210 feet (64 meters). The warming required to accomplish this would raise sea levels even more, because warmth makes water expand.

We would have two key options for handling the impact of rising sea levels:
1. Move, or
2. Protect.

Moving millions of people from the coasts would likely be the easiest. Even I don't like moving, but I would gladly move, if it meant saving millions of lives and civilization, too. Moving is not an easy option, but it might be far less costly than the second possible solution.

Protecting coastal populations would involve building dikes around those coastal areas. This is not the type of project you give to the lowest bidder, necessarily. Cutting corners on something like this could ultimately kill millions if shoddy workmanship or materials were to result in dike failures.

We need to assess the costs and benefits of both approaches—moving and protecting. How much would it cost to move New York City inland? If oceans continue to rise after all the glaciers are melted, would we have to move the city again? Could we develop a mobile strategy for coastal cities? How much would it cost to build a dike around the New York, New Jersey and Washington corridor? What would it cost to build canal locks into the dike to allow shipping?

Building a dike to surround San Francisco would not only save that city and its neighbors, but would also protect the valuable farming real estate of central California.

Island nations would disappear, or could be replaced by islands on pedestals.

But in all of this, we need to keep our attention on the end goal: protecting lives and civilization. Obviously, global cooling threatens billions of lives and civilization itself.

Warming threatens coastal real estate and the disruption of patterns (ocean currents, winds, commerce). But weighing inconveniences against deaths, it becomes clear that promoting global cooling to save coastal real estate is both lazy and genocidally selfish.

With global warming, some life might be threatened if it cannot move to a more desirable climate zone. This is where compassion could help transplant the life to a more compatible location.

Some people I've talked to actually think warming is causing mass extinctions. So far, I haven't seen any evidence to prove this. I have seen lots of evidence that industrial chemicals are causing disruptions and deaths amongst numerous species of plants and animals. Corporations are ruthless when it comes to protecting profits and only paying lip service to environmental concerns. And ironically, those people who shout the loudest against global warming are getting their news and information from those very same corporations they despise. The corporate names may be different, but the owners are the same.

The only way we can solve the truly big problems is to give up fear and self-concern. We have to stop reacting to the fear tactics of others. We have to approach the dangers with humility and calm resolve. We have to act with unconditional love, compassion, humble responsibility and fearless confidence; not react with self-concern, indifference, arrogant blame and fear.

Our largest stumbling block is in our own selfishness.

Chapter 17: Selflessness— Giving Up Self-Concern

"Catch him at the moment when he is really poor in spirit and smuggle into his mind the gratifying reflection, 'By jove! I'm being humble,' and almost immediately pride—pride at his own humility—will appear."—C. S. Lewis, The Screwtape Letters, 1942

Our world is endangered by rampant selfishness and self-concern. Those who have power want more of it. They are willing to kill for it. And they have gained experience from history showing how to kill with greater stealth. Popular entertainment has made criminality and evil more fashionable. Intelligence has become unpopular to the point where students purposefully get lower grades so they are not seen as "geeks" or worse. And people hold onto their viewpoints with greater arrogance and passion, because being "wrong" is too painfully uncomfortable.

Scientists are going along with the "warming catastrophe" hysteria, because they fear being ostracized by authorities who control funding. This tragedy of crime by inaction isn't affecting only climate science. Other fields are experiencing similar selfishness where scientists, researchers and doctors are going along with a popular lie so they can keep their jobs.

Each of these diseases contributes to the disease of *thermophobia*—the widespread fear of warmth. Every crime and every form of evil goes back to one simple attitude—self-concern. This is the heart of darkness. The great spiritual leaders of the past warned us about this.

We can solve the climate problems, but still end up destroying civilization and possibly all life on Earth, if we don't first handle this core problem.

How do you achieve perfect selflessness? One method is to satisfy selfishness and then to convert its desires to those of altruistic love. By this, you catch the very foundation of self-concern and upend it. This is the technique taught in the authentic Kabbalah of Bnei Baruch and the Ashlag Research Institute.

Albert Einstein once said, "A new type of thinking is essential if mankind is to survive and move toward higher levels" ("Atomic Education Urged by Einstein," *New York Times*, 1946:0525). A similar quote often attributed to Einstein, but for which a source has not been found, states, "The significant problems we face cannot be solved at the same level of thinking we were at when we created them." It has a similar meaning to the first quote and gives us an even more potent direction.

If you have darkness, you cannot cure it with more darkness; for that you require light. You cannot cure hatred with more hatred; for that, you need unselfish love. For this unnatural fear of warmth, you need compassionate understanding, but not sympathy. You need facts; not lies.

Every evil perpetrated in the history of humanity came from selfishness or self-concern. It's not impossible to give up self-concern, but it is difficult. A spiritual leader nearly two thousand years ago made this point abundantly clear.

Yehoshua of Nazareth said, "Enter by the narrow gate; for wide is the gate and broad is the way that leads to destruction, and there are many who go in by it. Because narrow is the gate and difficult is the way which leads to life, and there are few who find it.

"Beware of false prophets, who come to you in sheep's clothing, but inwardly they are ravenous wolves. You will know them by their fruits. Do men gather grapes from thornbushes or figs from thistles? Even so, every good tree bears good fruit, but a bad tree bears bad fruit. A good tree cannot bear bad fruit, nor can a bad tree bear good fruit. Every tree that does not bear good fruit is cut down and thrown into the fire. Therefore by their fruits you will know them.

"Not everyone who says to Me, 'Lord, Lord,' shall enter the kingdom of heaven, but he who does the will of My Father in heaven. Many will say to Me in that day, 'Lord, Lord, have we not prophesied in Your name, cast out demons in Your name, and done many wonders in Your name?' And then I will declare to them, 'I never knew you; depart from Me, you who practice lawlessness'" (Matthew 7:13–23, NKJV)!

When humanity finally matures, it will leave all manner of childish selfishness behind. But that might include only a small part of humanity. Not everyone desires to grow up.

Other books to consider:

'Shining a Light' series

Favorable Incompetence: Shining a Light on 9/11 by Rod Martin, Jr. How the official conspiracy theory is full of holes, and how that tragedy is becoming increasingly relevant.

Dirt Ordinary: Shining a Light on Conspiracies by Rod Martin, Jr. These days, the popular notion in America is that conspiracies are fantasies. Other places, not so much. But conspiracies are dirt ordinary with at least 489 new conspiracies starting every second, all day long, every day and all year long. This book puts the topic into the proper perspective, reveals the dangers of conspiracies and what we can do about them.

Climate Basics series

Climate Basics: Nothing to Fear by Rod Martin, Jr. Debunking the key claims of warming alarmists on climate change.

Deserts & Droughts: How does land ever get water? by Rod Martin, Jr. Expanding on the warming alarmist claim that global warming will lead to more droughts and deserts. Proving that the opposite is true.

More on Climate

Red Line — Carbon Dioxide: How humans saved all life on Earth by burning fossil fuels by Rod Martin, Jr. How 'climate change' and 'global warming' memes have been used to betray humanity.

Discount available on most ebook titles at
https://TharsisHighlands.WordPress.com.

Appendix

- References
- Glossary
- Videography
- Links to Illustrations
- About Rod Martin, Jr.
- Other Books
- Connect

References

Definitions from http://thefreedictionary.com/ unless otherwise noted.

Adam, David. (2007:1011). "Gore's climate film has scientific errors - judge." Retrieved on 2016:0116 from http://theguardian.com/environment/2007/oct/11/climatechange

Ashlag Research Institute. (2006:1108). "Perceiving Reality." http://perceivingreality.com/

Ball, Dr. Tim. (2015:1127). "An Important Lesson On The Anniversary of Climategate." Retrieved on 2016:0712 from https://wattsupwiththat.com/2015/11/27/an-important-lesson-on-the-anniversary-of-climategate/

Bastasch, Michael. (2015:0507). "NASA Warns About High CO2 Levels That Are Greening The Planet." Retrieved on 2016:0124 from http://dailycaller.com/2015/05/07/nasa-warns-about-high-co2-levels-that-are-greening-the-planet/

Bazell, Robert. (2010:1001). "U.S. apologizes for Guatemala STD experiments." Retrieved on August 8, 2016 from

http://nbcnews.com/id/39456324/ns/health-
sexual_health/t/us-apologizes-guatemala-std-
experiments/

Berko, J.; Ingram, D.; et al. (2014:0730). "Deaths Attributed to
Heat, Cold, and Other Weather Events in the United
States, 2006–2010." Retrieved on 2015:1112 from
http://cdc.gov/nchs/data/nhsr/nhsr076.pdf

Booker, Christopher. (2015:0301). "Dr Rajendra Pachauri: the
clown of climate change has gone." Retrieved on
2016:0712 from
http://telegraph.co.uk/comment/11441697/Dr-Rajendra-
Pachauri-the-clown-of-climate-change-has-gone.html

Brandt, Allan M. (1978:12). "Racism and Research: The Case of
the Tuskegee Syphilis Study." Retrieved on August 8,
2016 from
http://med.navy.mil/bumed/Documents/Healthcare%20
Ethics/Racism-And-Research.pdf

British Channel 4. (2007:0308). "The Great Global Warming
Swindle." Retrieved 2014:0830 from
https://youtube.com/watch?v=52Mx0_8YEtg

Bunch, Will. (2005:0831). "Why the Levee Broke." Retrieved
on 2015:1113 from
http://alternet.org/story/24871/why_the_levee_broke

Corbett, James. (2016:0131). "Meet Maurice Strong: Globalist,
Oiligarch, "Environmentalist." Retrieved on 2016:0709
from https://corbettreport.com/meet-maurice-strong-
globalist-oiligarch-environmentalist/

Corbett Report. (2009:1121). "Climategate: Dr. Tim Ball on the
hacked CRU emails." Retrieved on 2016:0708 from
https://youtube.com/watch?v=Ydo2Mwnwpac

Corbett Report. (2013:0927). "The IPCC Exposed." Retrieved
on 2016:0709 from
https://youtube.com/watch?v=LOyBfihjQvI

Council on Foreign Relations. (2016:0629). "A Conversation
    With John O. Brennan." Retrieved on 2016:0709 from
    https://youtube.com/watch?v=uIQDqxl9FtM
Deming, Dr. David. (2006:1206). "Statement of Dr. David
    Deming." Retrieved on 2016:0708 from
    http://epw.senate.gov/hearing_statements.cfm?id=2665
    43
Goddard, Steven. (2012:0712). "1988 : James Hansen And Tim
    Wirth Sabotaged The Air Conditioning In Congress."
    Retrieved on 2016:0618 from
    https://stevengoddard.wordpress.com/2012/07/12/1988-
    james-hansen-and-tim-wirth-sabotaged-the-air-
    conditioning-in-congress/
Goldenberg, Suzanne. (2014:0922). "Heirs to Rockefeller oil
    fortune divest from fossil fuels over climate change."
    Retrieved on 2016:0127 from
    http://theguardian.com/environment/2014/sep/22/rocke
    feller-heirs-divest-fossil-fuels-climate-change
GreenLearning. (2009:0625). "1 MILLION pounds of Food on 3
    acres. 10,000 fish 500 yards compost." Retrieved on
    2015:1113 from
    https://youtube.com/watch?v=jV9CCxdkOng
Griffin, G. Edward. (1994). The Creature from Jekyll Island: A
    Second Look at the Federal Reserve. American Media:
    Westlake Village, California
Grunwald, Michael. (2005:0908). "Money Flowed to
    Questionable Projects." Retrieved on 2015:1113 from
    http://washingtonpost.com/wp-
    dyn/content/article/2005/09/07/AR2005090702462.html
Hasegawa, H., Tada, R., et al. (2012:0823). "Drastic shrinking
    of the Hadley circulation during the mid-Cretaceous
    Supergreenhouse." Retrieved on 2015:1119 from
    http://clim-past.net/8/1323/2012/cp-8-1323-2012.pdf

Lüning, Sebastian. (2016:0109). "Evidence of the Medieval
    Warm Period in Australia, New Zealand and Oceania."
    Retrieved on 2016:0713 from
    https://wattsupwiththat.com/2016/01/09/evidence-of-
    the-medieval-warm-period-in-australia-new-zealand-
    and-oceania/
Martin, Jr., Rod. (2016). Dirt Ordinary: Shining a Light on
    Conspiracies. Tharsis Highlands: Cebu, Philippines
Mudelsee, M., et al, (2003:0911). "No upward trends in the
    occurrence of extreme floods in central Europe."
    Retrieved on 2016:0618 from
    http://nature.com/nature/journal/v425/n6954/full/nature
    01928.html
Mudelsee, M., et al. (2004:1202). "Extreme floods in central
    Europe over the past 500 years: Role of cyclone
    pathway 'Zugstrasse Vb'." Retrieved on 2016:0618 from
    http://onlinelibrary.wiley.com/doi/10.1029/2004JD00503
    4/full
NCDC. (ND). Graph: "Jan-Dec Global Mean Temperature
    over Land & Ocean." Retrieved 2015:1114 from
    http://ncdc.noaa.gov/sotc/service/global/global-land-
    ocean-mntp-anom/201001-201012.gif
NOAA. (ND). "U.S. Annual Count of EF-1+ Tornadoes, 1954
    through 2014." Retrieved 2015:1029 from
    http://www1.ncdc.noaa.gov/pub/data/cmb/images/torn
    ado/clim/EF1-EF5.png
NOAA. (ND). "U.S. Annual Count of Strong to Violent
    Tornadoes (F3+), 1954 through 2014." Retrieved
    2015:1029 from
    http://www1.ncdc.noaa.gov/pub/data/cmb/images/torn
    ado/clim/EF3-EF5.png

NSIDC. (ND). "Quick Facts on Ice Sheets." Retrieved on 2015:1113 from https://nsidc.org/cryosphere/quickfacts/icesheets.html

O'Connor, J.E., and Costa, J.E. (2004). "The World's Largest Floods, Past and Present: Their Causes and Magnitudes." Retrieved on 2016:0618 from http://pubs.usgs.gov/circ/2004/circ1254/pdf/circ1254.pdf

Paterson, W.S.B. (1972:11). "Laurentide Ice Sheet: Estimated Volumes during Late Wisconsin." Retrieved on 2015:1113 from http://onlinelibrary.wiley.com/doi/10.1029/RG010i004p00885/pdf

Pielke, Jr., Roger. (2014:0908). Tweet: "Phoenix floods, climate change!" Retrieved on 2016:0618 from https://twitter.com/RogerPielkeJr/status/509021248039313408/photo/1

Randerson, James. (2010:0127). "University in hacked climate change emails row broke FOI rules." Retrieved on 2016:0713 from https://theguardian.com/environment/2010/jan/27/uea-hacked-climate-emails-foi

Rose, David. (2015:0118). "Nasa climate scientists: We said 2014 was the warmest year on record... but we're only 38% sure we were right." Retrieved on 2016:0118 from http://dailymail.co.uk/news/article-2915061/Nasa-climate-scientists-said-2014-warmest-year-record-38-sure-right.html

Schneider, Mike. (2014:0103). "Florida Will Soon Have More People Than New York." Retrieved on 2015:1112 from http://businessinsider.com/florida-will-soon-have-more-people-than-new-york-2014-1

ScienceDaily.com. (2013:0708). "Deserts 'greening' from rising carbon dioxide: Green foliage boosted across the

world's arid regions." Retrieved on 2016:0124 from
http://sciencedaily.com/releases/2013/07/130708103521.
htm

Solomon, Lawrence. (2011:0103). "Lawrence Solomon: 97%
cooked stats." Retrieved on 2016:0127 from
http://business.financialpost.com/fp-
comment/lawrence-solomon-97-cooked-stats

Taylor, James. (2013:0710). "Global Warming? No, Satellites
Show Carbon Dioxide Is Causing 'Global Greening'."
Retrieved on 2016:0124 from
http://forbes.com/sites/jamestaylor/2013/07/10/global-
warming-no-satellites-show-carbon-dioxide-is-causing-
global-greening/

Wakefield, Dr. Andrew. (2016:0401). Vaxxed: From Cover-Up
to Catastrophe. Cinema Libre Studio: Burbank,
California

Wall Street Journal. (2009:1124). "Global Warming With the
Lid Off. The emails that reveal an effort to hide the
truth about climate science." Retrieved on 2016:0713
from
http://wsj.com/articles/SB10001424052748704888404574
547730924988354

Watts, Anthony. (2009:1122). "CRU Emails 'may' be open to
interpretation, but commented code by the
programmer tells the real story." Retrieved on
2016:0708 from
https://wattsupwiththat.com/2009/11/22/cru-emails-
may-be-open-to-interpretation-but-commented-code-
by-the-programmer-tells-the-real-story/

Watts, Anthony. (2009:1122). "Bishop Hill's compendium of
CRU email issues." Retrieved on 2016:0708 from
https://wattsupwiththat.com/2009/11/22/bishop-hills-
compendium-of-cru-email-issues/

Watts, Anthony. (2013:0411). "Evidence for a Global Medieval Warm Period." Retrieved on 2016:0713 from https://wattsupwiththat.com/2013/04/11/evidence-for-a-global-medieval-warm-period/

Watts, Anthony. (2013:0827). "Cook's 97% climate consensus paper crumbles upon examination." Retrieved on 2016:0127 from http://wattsupwiththat.com/2013/08/28/cooks-97-climate-consensus-paper-crumbles-upon-examination/

Watts, Anthony. (2013:1208). "The truth about 'We have to get rid of the medieval warm period'." Retrieved on 2016:0708 from https://wattsupwiththat.com/2013/12/08/the-truth-about-we-have-to-get-rid-of-the-medieval-warm-period/

Watts, Anthony. (2014:0908). "Phoenix flooding – not due to 'climate change', extreme rainfall events are not on the increase." Retrieved on 2016:0618 from https://wattsupwiththat.com/2014/09/08/phoenix-flooding-not-due-to-climate-change-extreme-rainfall-events-are-not-on-the-increase/

Watts, Anthony. (2014:1112). "Kashmir Floods Nothing New, Not Due To Climate Change." Retrieved on 2016:0618 from https://wattsupwiththat.com/2014/11/12/kashmir-floods-nothing-new-not-due-to-climate-change/

Watts, Anthony. (2015:1010). "USGS puts the kibosh on '1000 year flood' and 'caused by climate change' claims over South Carolina flooding." Retrieved on 2016:0618 from https://wattsupwiththat.com/2015/10/10/usgs-puts-the-kibosh-on-1000-year-flood-and-caused-by-climate-change-claims-over-south-carolina-flooding/

Watts, Anthony. (2016:0206). "Record Missouri flooding was manmade calamity, not climate change, scientist says."

Retrieved on 2016:0618 from
https://wattsupwiththat.com/2016/02/06/record-
missouri-flooding-was-manmade-calamity-not-climate-
change-scientist-says/

WattsUpWithThat.com. (2015:0120). "2014 The Most
Dishonest Year On Record." Retrieved on 2016:0119
from http://wattsupwiththat.com/2015/01/20/2014-the-
most-dishonest-year-on-record/

Waugh, Rob. (2011:1128). "Climategate scientists DID collude
with government officials to hide research that didn't
fit their apocalyptic global warming." Retrieved on
2016:0713 from
http://dailymail.co.uk/sciencetech/article-
2066240/Second-leak-climate-emails-Political-giants-
weigh-bias-scientists-bowing-financial-pressure-
sponsors.html

Glossary

Note: Not every term or concept has been included in this glossary. I encourage you to explore the subject online or in books on those terms for which you would like more information. Make learning a lifetime occupation.

carbon dioxide *n.*—an odorless, colorless gas and a minor constituent of the Earth's atmosphere. Without this trace gas, all life on Earth would die. Frequently abbreviated CO_2. This is what plants breathe. And plants "exhale" oxygen (which see). Not to be confused with poisonous carbon monoxide (CO).

climate *n.*—a persistent average state of a region's weather, typically taken over a period of several decades—usually thirty years.

climate change *n.*—modification of a region's persisting average weather. This can include warming or cooling, alterations in turbulence, patterns of flow, timing of events, atmospheric chemistry and more. Such modifications have occurred throughout the existence of our planet's atmosphere—more than 4 billion years. This term has been kidnapped by a modern movement to mean only "recent, manmade, warming and catastrophic" modifications to the atmosphere. This is a distortion of the original definition.

CO_2 *n.* —carbon dioxide (which see).

cryophilia *n.* —An attraction to or preference for cold (*cryo-*, cold, freezing; *-philia*, attraction to or preference for)

drought *n.* —a period of decreased rainfall that is insufficient for the life forms within a region. Drought typically occurs from changes in weather patterns, but more importantly from regional or global cooling. In fact, the global cooling of the last 50 million years or so has significantly desiccated the planet, increasing the extent of subtropical deserts and creating polar deserts.

Earth *n.* —our home planet. It possesses a breathable atmosphere, water in three key phases (solid, liquid, gas), dry land and a surface teeming with life. It also has one natural satellite typically called the Moon.

glacial *n.* —a cooler period of increased glaciation during an Ice Age in which polar glaciers expand to cover large portions of adjacent continents. During the last 1.1 million years of the current Ice Age, glacial periods have averaged 90,000 years in length (ref: W.S. Broecker, 1998). The duration of glacial periods for the last 800,000 years has varied between 24,000 and 143,000 years. Compare *interglacial*.

global cooling *n.* —a decrease in the average temperature of the planet. This can be a bad thing during our current Ice Age. Cooling tends to produce less evaporation, and thus drier climate.

global warming *n.* —an increase in the average temperature of the planet. This can be a good thing during our current Ice Age. Warming tends to produce more evaporation, and thus moister climate.

Holocene *n.* —an interglacial of the current Ice Age; the current interglacial (which see).

Holocene Optimum *n.* —a period of about 3,000 years wherein the northern hemisphere was as much as 1.1°C warmer than today. This warmth, compared with the shallow cool periods (roughly as warm as today) resulted in a green Sahara for about 3,000 years.

hurricane *n.* —A dangerous tropical cyclone of the Atlantic Ocean region. Compare *typhoon.*

Ice Age *n.* —a period of increased cooling where both polar regions experience permanent glaciation throughout the year. The current such period has had glaciation in Greenland and Antarctica for roughly 2.6 million years. Such periods include several glacial and interglacial periods, alternating between warmer and cooler phases.

interglacial *n.* —a warmer period of relaxed glaciation during an Ice Age in which polar glaciation recedes and global climate warms noticeably. The amount of warming and glacial receding can vary a great deal with some such periods being as much as 5°C warmer than our current Modern Warm Period, or 2°C cooler. There have been several dozen interglacials in the current Ice Age. For the last 1.1 million years, interglacials have averaged about 11,000 years in length (ref: W.S. Broecker, 1998). The duration of interglacial periods for the last 800,000 years has varied between 4,000 and 24,000 years. Compare *glacial.*

Intergovernmental Panel on Climate Change *n.* —a political organization associated with the United Nations tasked with determining the nature and extent of man's impact on the planetary climate as a result of burning fossil fuels.

IPCC *n.*—Intergovernmental Panel on Climate Change (which see).

Jupiter *n.*—the largest planet in our star system, roughly ten times the diameter of Earth, with a thick atmosphere many thousands of kilometers deep and no solid surface. Because of its great distance from the sun, it is extremely cold at the tops of the clouds, near the air pressure equivalent to that on Earth's surface. Despite the extreme cold, the planet hosts some of the largest storms in the solar system.

oxygen *n.*—a key constituent of Earth's atmosphere and the most vital gas for animal life. Animals exhale carbon dioxide (which see).

parts per million *n.*—the concentration of something as a fractional measure compared to a whole. If you take a million of something, the count given will be the number of pieces or portions out of that whole million that apply to a specific substance. This is similar to the term percent. Example: The atmosphere consists of 21 percent oxygen, or 210,000 parts per million oxygen.

Pleistocene *n.*—the current Ice Age (which see). This period of permanent polar glaciation has lasted for 2.6 million years. Before scientists knew very much about Earth's history, they thought the Pleistocene ended 11,600 years ago. Today, we know that the current epoch—the Holocene—is merely one in a series of dozens of interglacial periods that are part of this Ice Age.

ppm *abbr.*—parts per million (which see).

thermophobia *n.*— An abnormal fear of warmth or heat (*thermo-*, related to, caused by, or measuring heat or warmth; *-phobia*, an intense fear of or aversion to a specified thing)

tornado *n.*—a small, cyclonic storm, typically less than several hundred meters across, with extremely fast winds and an ability to create tremendous damage to buildings and to anything else above ground.

typhoon *n.*—a dangerous tropical cyclone of the Pacific Ocean region. Compare *hurricane*.

Venus *n.*—our sister planet, closer to the sun. The planet is slightly smaller than Earth (which see), has a crushing atmosphere of mostly CO_2, a heavily reflective cloud cover, and a surface with virtually no wind and temperatures hot enough to melt lead (462°C). The planet spins very, very slowly and has no natural satellite.

warm period *n.*—a span of time which has a higher temperature than the preceding and succeeding spans of time. Climate always changes and most frequently in repeating cycles. The Holocene has contained 10 clearly-defined major warm periods on a roughly 1,000-year cycle. Cycles of other periods make the pattern of warming and cooling more complex than they would be if there were only one cycle involved. The most recent four major warm periods of the Holocene have been, the Modern (1850 to today), the Medieval (850–1350), the Roman (200 BC–AD 100) and the Minoan (1400–1100 BC).

Videography

Be sure to Like, Comment and Subscribe to the channel:
https://youtube.com/c/RodMartinJr/

Climate Change Lies Exposed series

Top 10 Climate Change Lies Exposed
https://youtube.com/watch?v=ICGal_8qI8c
Climate Change Lie #1 Exposed: Global Warming is Bad
https://youtube.com/watch?v=KbfjEPo083U
Climate Change Lie #2 Exposed: CO2 Causes Dangerous
Global Warming
https://youtube.com/watch?v=ZH5ATcpMJQo
Climate Change Lie #3 Exposed: Global Warming Causes
Extreme Weather
https://youtube.com/watch?v=aTiBbAGl0qI
Climate Change Lie #4 Exposed: Global Warming causes
droughts
https://youtube.com/watch?v=DusZ5dP4hDw
Climate Change Lie #5 Exposed: Our current warmth is
unusual
https://youtube.com/watch?v=FR2aZc5bjUU

Climate Change Lie #6 Exposed: Our current level of CO2 is
unusually high
https://youtube.com/watch?v=ASV3UUwYZg0
Climate Change Lie #7 Exposed: The rate of warming is
dangerous
https://youtube.com/watch?v=OsJ67Hp4l-g
Climate Change Lie #8 Exposed: The Science is Settled
https://youtube.com/watch?v=6yzkAjWY8rM
Climate Change Lie #9 Exposed — There is a consensus on
dangerous, man made, Global Warming
https://youtube.com/watch?v=URE4NMk1DbA

Carbon Dioxide Fan Club

Earth vs. Venus: Will our world ever suffer runaway
greenhouse warming?
https://youtube.com/watch?v=SO1M8GEDyYk
Top 10 Facts that Prove CO2 Does NOT Drive Global
Temperature
https://youtube.com/watch?v=CSQlJx76b64
Verdict: CO2 Not Guilty! Greenhouse DESTROYED! Must see!
https://youtube.com/watch?v=1f6zB320Hac

Global Warming Fan Club

How Global Warming Made Civilization Possible
https://youtube.com/watch?v=057GgxpZWRc
Top 10 Reasons Global Warming is Good
https://youtube.com/watch?v=dQc4iXgrrEo

Big Climate Quiz (BCQ)

BCQ #1: Why didn't civilization start during the last glacial
period?
https://youtube.com/watch?v=Bf0gty2XAjw
BCQ #2: What Causes Wind to Blow?

https://youtube.com/watch?v=lhk7JIQ6e-U
BCQ #3: How does land ever get water?
https://youtube.com/watch?v=do0kb7Udq-g
BCQ #4: What is an Ice Age?
https://youtube.com/watch?v=RjMbE-G8JFo

Climate Music Video series

Thermophobia - Why Fear of Warming in the current Ice Age
is all wrong
https://youtube.com/watch?v=Q68fIkdC9Rk
Extreme Weather - How the Climate Change Alarm is All
Wrong
https://youtube.com/watch?v=x18gwLpLI2A
Thermophobia -- Debunking: "Global Warming causes more
storms"
https://youtube.com/watch?v=d40_2yGuV_o

Links to Illustrations

Introduction: Thermophobia in Perspective

Global population density map:
https://dropbox.com/s/euosfw6u68c6kro/earth_pop_by_lat.png?dl=0

Chapter 1: Unreasonable Fear

Global mean temperature over land & ocean, anomaly relative to 1901–2000:
https://ncdc.noaa.gov/sotc/service/global/global-land-ocean-mntp-anom/201401-201412.png

U.S. Annual Count of EF-1+ Tornadoes, 1954 through 2014:
http://www1.ncdc.noaa.gov/pub/data/cmb/images/tornado/clim/EF1-EF5.png

U.S. Annual Count of Strong to Violent Tornadoes (F3+), 1954 through 2014:
http://www1.ncdc.noaa.gov/pub/data/cmb/images/tornado/clim/EF3-EF5.png

Chapter 8: The Real Culprit Behind Climate Change

Air temperature at summit of Greenland ice sheet 10,700 years (modified) showing 10 warm periods, plus graph of CO_2 levels:
https://dropbox.com/s/bif07lpubyn2ztl/10%2C700_Years_GISP 2_w_CO2_modified.png?dl=0

Temperature anomaly over the last 450,000 years of current Ice Age, including most recent 5 interglacials:
http://climate4you.com/images/VostokTemp0-420000%20BP.gif

About Rod Martin, Jr.

Rod Martin, Jr. is a modern polymath (Renaissance man)—artist, scientist, mathematician, engineer and philosopher. He first became interested in climate science in the mid-70s. A forest ecology PhD friend of his was retiring and donated two climate texts to the cause. Initially, his interest in the subject covered planetary atmospheres—weather systems, atmospheric retention rates, optical thickness (greenhouse effect), adiabatic lapse rates, climate chemistry and planetary habitability.

Like so many others, during the 70s, 80s and 90s, Martin's interest in ecology and the environment continued to grow. When Al Gore's film, An Inconvenient Truth, came out in 2006, Martin was an immediate fan. But as the controversy on the topic heated up, Martin suddenly realized that all of the things he had learned about climate over the years contradicted many of the so-called facts in Gore's award-winning film.

In college, from the mid-90s to the early 2000s, Martin studied computer science, earning a degree, *summa cum laude.*

With only a 139 IQ, Martin realized that he was not the sharpest implement in the tool shed. In fact, all of his younger brothers had far higher IQs. From this relative handicap, he learned the immense value of humility and the need to remain unattached to any ideas, lest they become dogma, and blind him from further discovery. Thus, he was able to learn the true value of skepticism, and was able to recognize the inevitable pitfalls of that scientific paradigm. He also made the distinction between confidence in knowledge (an enormous source of blindness) and confidence in one's ability to find new knowledge (a source of empowerment).

In 2016, Martin implemented a campaign to set the record straight on climate. He wasn't alone. Many climate scientists, astrophysicists, meteorologists and concerned citizens had already begun to speak out against the so-called "scientific consensus" (an oxymoron, because science is never done by consensus). Martin has created numerous educational videos on climate change and global warming and created a website to discuss these topics in greater detail. **https://GlobalWarmthBlog.WordPress.com/**

From a lasting love of stars and astronomy, he created 3D space software, "Stars in the NeighborHood," available online. **https://SpaceSoftware.WordPress.com/buy-now/**

He currently resides in the Philippines with his wife, Juvy.

He has taught mathematics, information technology, critical thinking and professional ethics at Benedicto College, Mandaue City, Cebu. He continues to teach online and to write.

Other Books by Rod Martin, Jr.

Non-Fiction (as Rod Martin, Jr.)

The Art of Forgiveness, Tharsis Highlands (2012, 2015)
The Bible's Hidden Wisdom: God's Reason for Noah's Flood,
   Tharsis Highlands (2014)
The Spark of Creativity, Tharsis Highlands (2014)
Dirt Ordinary: Shining a Light on Conspiracies, Tharsis
   Highlands (2015)
Favorable Incompetence: Shining a Light on 9/11, Tharsis
   Highlands (2015)
Thermophobia: Shining a Light on Global Warming, Tharsis
   Highlands (2016)
*Red Line — Carbon Dioxide: How humans saved all life on Earth by
   burning fossil fuels*, Tharsis Highlands (2016)
*The Science of Miracles: How Scientific Method Can Be Applied to
   Spiritual Phenomena*, Tharsis Highlands (2018)
Proof of God, Tharsis Highlands (2018)
Deserts & Droughts: How does Land Ever Get Water?, Tharsis
   Highlands (2018)
*Taking Charge: How to Assert Positive Control Over Your Own
   Emotions*, Tharsis Highlands (2018)

*Spirit is Digital—Science is Analog: Discovering where miracles
and logic intersect,* Tharsis Highlands (2019)
Proof of Atlantis? Evidence of Plato's Lost Island Empire, Tharsis
Highlands (2019)
*Enemies of Christ: The Need to Protect Our Own Salvation from
Ravening Wolves,* Tharsis Highlands (2019)

Science Fiction (as Carl Martin)

Touch the Stars: Emergence, with John Dalmas, Tor (1983),
expanded Tharsis Highlands (2012)
Touch the Stars: Diaspora, Book 2 of Touch the Stars, Tharsis
Highlands (2014)
Entropy's Children, anthology of short fiction, Tharsis
Highlands (2014)
Gods and Dragons, Book 1 of *Edge of Remembrance,* Tharsis
Highlands (2017)
Tales of Atlantis Lost, Book 2 of *Edge of Remembrance,* Tharsis
Highlands (2017)

Excerpt from
Dirt Ordinary: Shining a Light on Conspiracies

Introduction: Conspiracies are Dirt Ordinary

Bright green flooded the space between buildings, and the
December sun poured down upon metropolitan Cebu. Inside
the solitary structure of a modern, four-year college, classes of
students ignored the heat beyond their air-conditioned rooms.

One of those students asked a provocative question of
his American professor—your author—about politics in the
United States. I admitted that there had been some evidence of
corruption in America. I gave Watergate as an example.

"Was that a conspiracy?" asked the student.

For a moment, something shifted in my mind. I felt a
knot in my stomach, a subtle tightness across my body,

combined with a brief urge to flee. I felt the awkwardness of exposure, without knowing its source.

The next moment, I became critically aware of those feelings. A sense of anxiety faded as I looked inward at my own thoughts.

I had become aware of an automatic response to the word "conspiracy"—a knee-jerk reaction that took me entirely by surprise.

"Yes," I replied. "That incident was a perfect example of a conspiracy and the crime which followed."

Over the next few months, I had the good fortune to explore this topic even further. In my professional ethics class for college seniors, I observed that none of my students had my reaction to the word or topic. Was this merely a personal weakness on my part—a flaw in my own character?

Was my reaction an anomaly? Or was it purely an American phenomenon?

In my class preparation, I came across the videos of a researcher who had experienced something similar. He had found that the citizens of Europe and some Third World countries were equally relaxed with the conspiracy concept, while Americans suffered an automatic block on the subject.

Many Americans claimed to be skeptics, while ridiculing anyone who talked of such things, but those supposed skeptics showed none of the restraint and humility of a true scientist. In America, ridicule of conspiracy talk had become habitual (Storm Clouds Gathering).

I poured over dozens of hours of YouTube videos. More than once, I saw newscasters and show hosts roll their eyes at the mention of some controversial topic.

One acerbic host wouldn't wait for his guest to finish speaking. He would lambaste his guest with something like, You nut! You're a loony toon—tin-foil conspiracy crackpot.

Throughout the worst of them, what distressed me most was the non-sequitur nature of the hosts' responses. A guest might mention a controversial fact or raise a provocative question, but all too frequently, these were referred to as "conspiracy theories."

Were the hosts so unintelligent that they didn't know the difference between theory and fact, or conspiracy and question? Had show hosts become so blind and belligerent that they could not ask for clarification? Was this some group delusion that had come to grip the American news media? Or was their some natural or artificial force molding their attitudes and speech?

It might prove helpful to find answers to these questions, but we won't be answering them in this book. We will, however, look at the common nature of conspiracies. We will show that ridicule is not warranted, at least most of the time. Some conspiracy theories are based on facts, instead of imagination or delusion. These days, however, the corporate media has made it fashionable to ridicule facts, questions and even the search for truth.

It should be noted that a suspicious nature is only paranoia if it is unreasonable—based upon delusion or imagination. If suspicions are based upon facts, that is an entirely different animal. More and more, all suspicions are called "paranoia" in error. Both movies and corporate media are feeding this inaccurate view of things. And the public who view these movies and media repeat that behavior so that it becomes a self-reinforcing phenomenon. Another important question not to be covered in this book involves the reason why movies so consistently refer to all suspicion as paranoia. Is it by accident? A new social norm for the definition? Where did that norm crop up? Who originated it and why? Suspicion

= paranoia = insanity. This false chain of equalities is inadvertently creating a kind of blindness.

The Cost of Conspiracies

In the twentieth century, documented conspiracies resulted in the deaths of 142.2 million people. This includes every major, and many minor wars throughout that hundred year period. But that's only for wars. Millions of other deaths have resulted from corporate conspiracies, gang and organized crime conspiracies and many other types of conspiracies.

But what really are conspiracies? Quite simply, they are conversations. A conspiracy happens when two or more people talk about doing something unethical or illegal. Like all evil, the perpetrators want their plans to remain shrouded in darkness, until at least the plan is so well along that nothing can stop it. Even then, the perpetrators frequently want to protect their own carcasses from prosecution.

For instance, Hitler might not have been successful in taking over the German government so thoroughly, if everyone suddenly knew that the Reichstag fire had been created by his own thugs, instead of a lone Communist patsy....

https://tharsishighlands.wordpress.com/books/dirt-ordinary-conspiracies/

Connect with Rod Martin, Jr.

Rod Martin, Jr. is his pen name for non-fiction. Carl Martin is his pen name for fiction.
BitChute—https://bitchute.com/channel/M63WrjRpNSPT/
Minds—https://minds.com/RodMartinJr
Gab—https://gab.ai/RodMartinJr
Website and Blog—https://rodmartinjr.wordpress.com/
HubPages—https://hubpages.com/@lone77star
Smashwords author page—
      https://smashwords.com/profile/view/CarlMartin77
Smashwords author page—
      https://smashwords.com/profile/view/RodMartinJr
Udemy courses page—https://udemy.com/user/rodmartinjr/
Facebook—https://facebook.com/RodMartinJr/
Twitter—https://twitter.com/LoneStar77/
YouTube—https://youtube.com/c/RodMartinJr/
Goodreads author page—https://goodreads.com/Carl_Martin
Goodreads author page—
      https://goodreads.com/Rod_Martin_Jr
Amazon author page—https://amazon.com/Carl-Martin/e/B008CX8KN6/

Amazon author page—https://amazon.com/Rod-Martin-Jr/e/B008CZ9JTS/

Made in the USA
Lexington, KY
06 September 2019